Cincinnati...
For Pete's Sake

Dedicated to my beautiful wife, Kathy, and my beloved children, Liz and James.

Cover: Ron Huff. Photos: Michael Keating, Steven M. Herppich, Joseph Fuqua II.

Cincinnati...

For Pete's Sake

A collection of Cincinnati Enquirer Columnist

Peter Bronson's greatest hits

By Peter Bronson

Chilidog Press
PMB 182
1081-B State Route 28
Milford, Ohio 45150-2199
www.peterbronson.com

First printing, 2003

ISBN 0-9740602-0-8

LCCN 2003092847

Contents:

Introduction: Just buy it, for Pete's sake

Writing a column is like riding in a rodeo. Some days you just hang on with white knuckles and hope you don't fall off and get stomped by 2,000 pounds of angry bull.

Other days it's like rearranging the furniture in front of 200,000 people. Everyone wants to tell you where the couch goes, and offer helpful tips and suggestions, such as, "Your brain is tilting a little bit too far to the right." Then when you get it just right and everyone is applauding, an editor comes in and sets the couch on fire.

And sometimes, just once in awhile, being a columnist allows me to play middleman to minor miracles. It allows me to help readers like Tom, the car dealer, find Cubie, the guy who just lost his wife in a car wreck and can't afford to pay for a funeral. Then Tom opens his heart and his checkbook, and a very sad story is just a little bit less heartbreaking because an ordinary guy has demonstrated what Jesus asked us to do: "Love your neighbor as yourself."

Most of the time, it's more like being the teacher's assistant with the taped glasses in high school, who thought he was some kind of janitor VIP because he got to carry a big fat ring of keys and operate the film projecter during "Textiles on Parade" and other film classics that put us to sleep and caused premature senility. Columnists get lots of keys to interesting places, then try to show where they've been without boring readers to death.

Of course, my columns are much more interesting than "Aluminum is Your Friend" and the other movies teachers inflicted on us when they came to work with a hangover. Of course they are.

At least, that's what I'm hoping with this book.

I'm hoping people will spend $20 for a book of my favorite columns from the Cincinnati Enquirer. And if you are reading this far, chances are, you've already bought the book. So let me tell you what's inside.

Most of the columns are about Cincinnati, the city I have come to know and love since I moved here from Tucson in 1992. But most of them are not "news" that has turned moldy like boxes of leftover pizza under the bed in a dorm-room. I have included columns in which I reported news. But I only included the stories that still have something to say to us about where our city is, how it got here, and where it's going.

These columns do not have any "best if used by yesterday" freshness date. They have the timeless ability to resist decay like a Slim Jim that oozes preservatives.

I've always thought the best columns are the ones about life. And that covers a lot of real estate far beyond Cincinnati. That takes in our nation. Our history. Cops on the beat and politicians on the make. Heroes and villains. Special times we share. The fears and joys that affect us all. Our families, friends and that topic that seems to be taboo in so many newsrooms – faith.

These are the things that really matter long after we've forgotten why we were so twisted in knots over the big scandal of the week a year ago.

Just about any reporter can write a news story better than I can. The job of a columnist is to give that news a meaning that puts the "me" in media for each reader. The job of a columnist is to make metaphorical house calls, to stop by and visit like a friend and talk about the things that matter with humor, interesting insights, some intelligence and, most of all, honesty.

The highest compliment to a columnist, right after, "I put it on the refrigerator," is "You call it like you see it." If this comes from people who start out by saying, "I don't always agree with you, but. . ." – then that means I have passed the test of integrity. I believe readers can see through a phony all the way across the rodeo ring. Why take the falls and bite the dust just to wave your hat around for a short ride if your heart's not in it?

Going back through all my old columns to select the ones for this book was like a reunion with old friends. I chose a special chapter of Christmas columns, because I learned to love the written word as a boy, on Christmas Eves, when my mother would drag out old newspaper clippings of our favorite Christmas-story columns, and we would all gather around to read and listen. If that happens to any of my columns, this book is a success.

And if you've read this far and haven't made up you mind – just buy it, For Pete's Sake.

*"Welcome to
Cincinnati — now
go back to Arizona."*

March 14, 1999

Treasures in our attic

Archaeologists say there must be hundreds of undiscovered tombs in Egypt's Valley of the Kings, and any one of them could be more spectacular than the gold-plated mausoleum where high priests jarred up the remains of a boy-Pharaoh named Tut.

I picture those sealed rooms sleeping in silent darkness for thousands of years, patiently waiting for the groan of shifting stones and the blinding shaft of dust-sparkled sunlight that will signal the first returning footsteps of human life.

Sort of like Cincinnati's downtown after 7 p.m., when all the slaves who toil in our skyline pyramids lay down their ropes, whips and pry-poles, stop pushing huge stone blocks over each other and flee to surrounding villages until the sun rises again.

On a Sunday morning, downtown's valley of business kings does a pretty good impression of Egypt: Towering tombs of banking, insurance, government and industry sit sphinxlike in geometric shadows, looking down imperiously at puny mortals, asking an unanswerable riddle:

What mark will this civilization leave in 4,000 years?

When they brush the dust away from buried keyboards, fax machines and cell phones, will they say we worshiped treasure or trash?

Fortunately, we don't have to wait that long to find jewels left behind by previous generations who have built and rebuilt our city.

I found one the other day on Elm Street, just a few blocks from the Enquirer's pyramid. Just north of Seventh Street, behind gray stone walls and wooden doors arched like a bishop's hat, is a symphony of stained glass, scarlet velvet and carved walnut called Covenant-First Presbyterian Church. Its roots reach deep into Cincinnati soil, as part of six churches that date back to 1790. The black-coffee pews on Elm Street were first filled on April 11, 1875.

And here's a secret:

Each Wednesday at noon, the round, plum-shaped song of a 1,700-pound tower bell cast by Paul Revere invites anyone who is passing by to join a short lunchtime service. The slow, solemn chant of the bell somehow manages to sound near and far at the same time, like the world outside the heavy church doors.

It seems to speak the prayer written on the "Inspiration at Noon" bulletin:

"Come now, little man! Flee for awhile from your tasks, hide yourself for a little space from the turmoil of your thoughts. For a little while, give yourself to God, and rest in Him for a little." — St.

9

Anselm, 1033-1109 A.D.

When the church bell's final echoes fade, the deep-throated, two-story pillars of a golden pipe organ fill the cavernous sanctuary as if giving voice to the sunlight spilling through deep ruby, yellow, royal blue and green stained glass.

Pastor Theodore Kalsbeek leads a call to worship. A hymn is sung. A soloist performs. A speaker shares brief remarks.

Bread for the soul, food for thought, nourishment for the spirit — all in just 30 minutes, with time left for lunch ($3 for soup, sandwich and a slice of delicious homemade pie).

I was invited to stand in the pulpit at Covenant-First Presbyterian Church last Wednesday. The view was inspiring. Breathtaking. A spiritual battery boost.

Standing there, I wondered what sermons had flashed from that same pulpit like thunderbolts on a dark prairie, what prayers had been sent in silent hope and desperation to the beamed ceiling high above, what tears of joy and grief had fallen like dew on the red carpet.

Compared to that, my remarks were "just add hot water" instant cup-a-soup.

I suppose there are other churches downtown that are just as beautiful, with similar programs to minister to downtown workers.

After almost seven years of strolling the streets, I've hardly begun to explore unopened trunks in the downtown attic.

I've seen hotel rooms that fit a detective's description from a Raymond Chandler novel — splashy floral curtains, art-deco elevators, claw-footed tubs and leaded mirrors that look back at you from 1940 and make a man feel undressed without a fedora.

There are peaceful spots on the riverbank where Huck and Jim could sit chewing stalks of grass and watch the Ohio slide downstream like time itself.

There must be hundreds of undiscovered treasures in the valleys of downtown Cincinnati. And when archaeologists dig them up thousands of years from now, I hope they judge us by Covenant-First Presbyterian, as well as our monuments to worldly wealth.

Honk if You Can't Drive

First, let me stipulate that I am not the world's greatest driver.

Making such a confession is unmanly. It's probably even un-American. But despite repeated, er, "refresher" courses in driver's training, at the invitation of various law enforcement agencies, I remain a recidivist speeder and occasional hazard to mailboxes, slow squirrels and people who drive defenselessly.

At one session of traffic safety school in Arizona, the instructor asked if anyone would admit to being a below-average driver. I raised my hand.

Now, I figured I wouldn't be there if I was perfect, so I might as well admit my errors and maybe they would let me go. I assumed that most of the other 50 adults did not exactly volunteer for remedial traffic-safety school or win free tuition by having spotless driving records.

But mine was the only hand that went up. It stuck out there all alone like a defendant rising for sentencing, while my classmates gave me those smug looks you get from other drivers who rocket past while the police write you a ticket.

I was stunned. I looked at the DUI offender in the Anthrax T-shirt next to me. Then I looked at the woman across the table who had been overheard muttering before class, "Hey, I flashed my lights at that guy with the white cane. He shoulda stayed on his curb." I glanced at the elderly man I'd seen pulling into several spaces in the parking lot, with a motor scooter stuck in the giant grille of his 1974 Olds Vista Cruiser. And I thought: If everyone else in this room is "above average," what does that make me?

I felt like the worst driver in the world. But then I moved to Cincinnati.

Here, I feel right at home. Sometimes, I even dare to feel above average.

I felt above average the time I watched a Marlboro cowboy in a jacked-up, four-wheel-drive pickup furiously spinning his earth-mover tires and slowly sliding sideways off a slippery street while I passed him by in my lowly sedan.

My driving vocabularly was definitely way above average the night it took me nearly four hours to drive 20 miles on I-71, because so many Cincinnati drivers panicked at the sight of "Sleet From Outerspace!" — and aimed straight for the nearest ditch.

I know I'm nothing like those average Cincinnati drivers, who are so steady and reliable. They choose a lane and stick to it — no matter what. You could try to merge into their lane with a convoy of the First Armored Division, and they wouldn't move over if they had 24 empty lanes to use.

Not me. I use all the lanes, every chance I get.

And I'm nothing like those other average Cincinnati drivers who seem so relaxed and spontaneous. Forget that exit? No problemo. They just swerve across three or four lanes of traffic, and get off before anyone blames them for all those wrecks that seem to keep happening in their rearview mirrors.

Not me. I always get blamed.

But every time I survive a coronary panic stop on the freeway so some gawker can slam on his brakes to get a closer look at a minor fender bender on the other side of the road, I think: "Hey, I'm a better driver than that. I'd never slow down for a wreck — not even my own. I've seen crumpled steel and broken headlights plenty of times. Big deal."

And nothing makes me feel exceptionally above average like a little bit of snow. Just enough to cover a dime will bring your average Cincinnati drivers to a screeching halt and make a practical joke of the term "rush hour traffic."

Not me. I learned to drive in Michigan, which is a tall Indian word for "winter wasteland of snow up to HERE." And everyone in Michigan knows that the proper way to drive in anything less than 28 inches of snow is to floor it and get home before it gets really deep.

What Cincinnati calls a big snow is what Michigan calls "summer." That so-called storm last week may have paralyzed Cincinnati, but it was not what anyone north of the sanity border would call a "real snow."

A real snow is the kind that closes down the radio stations before they can tell you if the schools are closed.

A real snow is the kind that is so deep, the National Guard gets stuck trying to clear a path for the snow plows.

A real snow is not measured by inches — it's measured by the number of streetlights you can change without a ladder.

A real snow is the kind I saw once in Northern Michigan, when I couldn't even find my office to go to work because it was buried in a snowdrift.

Sometimes I wish that would happen here.

I may not be the world's greatest driver, but I know one thing better than the average Cincinnati driver: when to leave my car parked in the garage.

May 29, 1994

Living on the fault line

I have this theory about Cincinnati's Richter-scale social earthquakes: We're sitting smack on the middle of a cultural fault line that separates ordinary, corn-fed Midwesterners from the lotus-eaters and lunatics on each coast.

So when Marge Schott says guys who wear earrings look like fruits, the tectonic plate that connects us to East Coast Political Correctness shudders and shrinks back in horror. But regular folks who live here just nod and say, "Uh-hunh. Go gettum, Marge."

When the sheriff tries to close down Poor Super Man, because it has nothing to do with caped crusaders, but is actually an artsy play about Guys Wrestling in Bed With Their Pants Off, the geological plate connected to Do What You Like California buckles and sways like a collapsing freeway. But locals scratch their heads and wonder: "Since when does Superman wear earrings? Whatkinda sicko would pay to see that?"

When the aftershocks subside, Cincinnati feels like an urban nerd again: the city that wore white socks to the prom.

Instead of recognizing uncommonly good common sense for what it is, our West Coast wannabes and pseudo-sophisticates shake their heads and mutter the ultimate putdown: "Only in Cincinnati."

Well, there's an upside to life on the fault line. It means we're as far as we can get from the Rotten Apple and L.A. Lawless. And that means good things also happen "Only in Cincinnati."

Such as:

It's a summer Sunday morning and we're trying to decide what to do with a houseful of friends from Michigan when a light bulb goes on: Let's go downtown.

Our guests go ashen-faced with fear. To someone from a state terrorized by Detroit, the idea of going downtown without an armed escort when it's not a matter of life and death sounds as suicidal as a walking tour of Sarajevo.

Imagine their surprise. They marvel at Cincinnati's historic architecture, smiling faces and panhandler-free streets like prisoners on parole. Even I'm impressed. I work in it every day, but downtown on its day off is different. It's Sunday sneakers comfortable. Even the shadows are softer. Kids play in the fountain. Strangers smile and nod. Buttery sunlight melts down past vacant office windows onto wide-open sidewalks where families stroll aimlessly.

Downtown with its coat and tie off is a cross between business and pleasure — Pomp and

Circumstance on a steel guitar, a briefcase on a beach. Turning Fountain Square into a public living room feels like hijacking Riverfront Stadium for a softball game.

A few months later, our friends call about visiting again. They don't even mention Kings Island. They want to go back downtown: "Let's have brunch at that hotel you showed us."

Eat your heart out, Los Angeles.

I'm on a crowded elevator heading home one Friday, when two women get on and one announces, "It's Kelly's birthday." Suddenly everyone sings a chorus of "Happy Birthday."

The elevator stops. We all get off, laughing. Try to picture it in Manhattan.

It's Take Your Daughter to Work Day, and my 12-year-old and I have decided to lunch at Arnold's so we can walk past the hole in the ground that will be the Whatshisname Arts Center.

We are enjoying our lunch until the waitress sees my credit card on the table and says, "Sorry, we don't take plastic, it's cash or checks only" — as she drops a bill that is $4 more than I have in my no-checkbook wallet.

One of us at the table is naive enough to be terrified that owner Jim Tarbell will put us in shackles and force us to wash dishes. But my daughter is unfazed.

Just as I am about to fall to my knees and beg for mercy, a man approaches the table. "I couldn't help overhearing," he says discreetly. "I don't mean to insult you, but would you like to borrow five bucks?"

I am about as insulted as a man in quicksand grabbing a rope. I take the fiver — along with his address to pay him back — and we leave smiling:

"Only in Cincinnati."

Cincinnati can be audaciously corny — a place where family values are a way of life, not a Hollywood debate. A place where people still have the basic decency to be shocked to the bones by the killing of a young woman. A place where real heroes rushed to help and comfort Maria Olberding; where Sean Kasselman grabbed a gun from his car and ran down her attacker. A place where Maria's parents expressed their sorrow for the family of the 16-year-old boy accused of killing her.

Cincinnati is an overgrown Mayberry. We have our city council that acts like Otis the town drunk; our Barney Fife Behavior Police; our Gomers shouting, "Citizen's arrest."

But somehow, the Andy Taylor side of the city seems to come up with the right answer at the end of every episode.

That's something sturdy to hang onto during the next social earthquake.

May 10, 1998

See you in church

My unscientific survey of the Cincinnati Yellow Pages discovered that churches outnumber golf courses by six to one. That's good news. I mean really good news, brothers and sisters. Can I hear an amen?

On any given Sunday, more than 1,200 churches worship, praise, pray and sing to God, each in its own voice.

The doors are open. You can choose a church named New Thought, New Life or Word of Life. You can choose God's Almighty Restoration and Deliverance, the Anointed Church of the Living God or the Revealed Holiness House of God.

Just don't choose to throw away a perfectly good Sunday counting and cursing the number of times you hit a ball with a stick. Don't choose to stay smug and snug in your own safe sanctuary, without ever visiting another. If you do, you will miss a lot.

I've been attending a different church each Sunday since my daughter was assigned to explore new churches for a high school class. So far, I have learned that what I know about the various ways people worship could fit on a communion wafer, with room left over for the Book of Psalms.

But I have also learned that it doesn't matter. Churches are like trumpets, French horns, cymbals, violins, flutes and pipe organs in God's orchestra, each playing different notes in the same heavenly symphony.

At Good Shepherd Catholic Church on Kemper Road, the huge sanctuary overflows with Casual Fridays Catholics in Dockers and polo shirts. In a suit and tie, I felt like a pallbearer at a pool party.

There were no "kneelers," but some Catholics still dip in that direction, just as the casual-but-neat service made a bow toward traditional Catholic rituals.

As a visitor, I sometimes felt like a rookie line-dancer at a cowboy bar. But the priest's message was as clear as holy water: "Thomas, because thou hast seen me, thou hast believed: blessed are they that have not seen, and yet have believed." (John 21:29)

A week later at St. James Orthodox Christian Church, we stepped into an old brick schoolhouse near Loveland, and walked into the Holy Land, taken back to the time of Christ by a priest whose authority flows in a direct line from the apostles. Clouds of exotic incense swirled around Byzantine icons, reflecting a golden glow from a chorus of candles. The Mass was chanted more than spoken, in a hypnotic sing-song of Greek and Arabic, with brief interruptions of English. It was a place layered in ancient mystery. Rituals left behind by Good Shepherd were thick in the air at St. James, like the smoky brimstone breath of God.

In some churches, sermons are punctuated by "hallelujahs" or stand-up applause. In this one, a phrase echoed through the centuries, telling of faith everlasting: "Always and ever and unto ages of ages."

On the third Sunday, we went to Solid Rock Church off I-75, south of Middletown.

I could feel the energy when we entered the sanctuary — a vast room with a blue neon dove on the ceiling, drawing our eyes to the stage-altar, where a chorus bigger than some congregations lifted us to our feet on mighty wings of joy.

This place rocks the Holy Ghost.

I expected one of those churches I've seen in movies that mock religion — men in sculpted TV-preacher hair and women in Tammy Faye makeup. But it wasn't Hollywood. It was the real deal — a racially integrated, friendly, uninhibited congregation that knows how to worship, heart and soul.

If you can imagine Aretha Franklin with a gospel choir, backed up by kicking music, you can imagine why people drive two hours for a spiritual battery boost at Solid Rock. "If one soul is saved, all of heaven dances," guest minister Carol Kornacki shouted. Four people came forward — and the place rocked and rolled with prayers of praise and thanks.

Message of the day: "God is soooo cooool."

There are churches like wax museums, where people treat worship as a spectator sport. When they're not watching their neighbors, they watch their watches.

There are churches that believe Jesus was a Democrat; and some that think God is a Republican.

And then there are churches that are no longer wilting on the vine — they are blooming like wild mustard, spreading seeds of faith on the wind.

I love the warm and close-knit, farm-kitchen community of my church, Loveland Presbyterian. But discovering all these new churches is like stumbling onto a hidden library of great books by my favorite author.

According to my survey, visitors are not just allowed — they are welcome. Imagine that. Instead of being a day that divides us by race, income and denomination, every Sunday can be an adventure in faith.

God is soooo cooool.

Can I hear an Amen?

Four walls don't make a home

If walls could talk, could they tell us how many dreams have been drowned in public housing? How many hopes have been smothered as they slept by the crushing burden of impersonal poverty?

Apartment 16C on Heath Court at English Woods is empty. A fresh coat of unconcerned beige covers layers of paint like tree rings for each family that moved in and out.

Ancient hardwood floors are varnished the color of beer in a glass, scarred by scuffs and stains like initials carved in a desktop.

The bedroom closets have no doors. It's a fitting metaphor for the 700 "units" at English Woods, which are less homes than letter slots — numbered boxes behind little locked doors in long brick buildings that look like old post offices.

A tiny kitchen is paved in mental-hospital linoleum, with a 1960s stove crouching against a wall. The smell is a mix of stale air, cockroaches and futility. The windows look out onto yards that seem beaten down. Stick-figure saplings are dwarfed by extra-large Dumpsters outside each door to reduce the litter that skitters across parking lots and infiltrates the surrounding woods like an encamped army of milk cartons and disposable diapers.

Some people think the "projects" are trashed by people who don't care. I've always wondered if the people are trashed by housing that doesn't care.

If homes can be ruined by radon and other "environmental hazards," isn't it possible that the walls in a public housing apartment can get so saturated with misery that they are no longer fit for human habitation?

Sadness seeps out of every surface. Anyone with a heart can sense it. Here is the scene of marriages, babies, first days of school, lovemaking, family dinners, carefully packed school lunches, quarrels, drinking, wife beatings, divorces, anger, loneliness, failure, drugs, fear and random killings of the human spirit.

How many children have pressed tear-stained cheeks to the glass and wondered why they were born to this?

Doctors, judges and business leaders have lived here, I am told. It's a testimony to the triumph of the human spirit. But for each one who struggled to the surface and gulped the sweet air of success, how many sank to the bottom?

English Woods was built in 1942, as part of a strategy to dam up ponds of poor people that could be managed like a flood-control project. It reached its acme of cruel compassion in the 1960s

"Great Society."

Bulldoze it all. Bury the foundations and scatter the bricks.

The Cincinnati Metropolitan Housing Authority wants to level English Woods and build new homes for the poor, side-by-side with homes that go on the market: For Sale — city views, close to downtown. Poor families could rent and gradually own homes next door to neighbors who inhale hope and exhale ambition like the ordinary air they breathe. That would do more for the poor than all the sanctimonious boycotters combined.

I've seen the new homes CMHA is selling at City West. They have airy, open floor plans and smell like joint compound and fresh-cut lumber — the new-car smell of a home that has never been lived in.

The walls are as crisp and white as a clean sheet of paper — a place to begin a family story.

Learning to love Cincinnati

When I fell off a turnip truck in Cincinnati eight years ago, I felt like I was a prisoner in a chain gang: another Cool Hand Luke who failed to outwit the bloodhounds, dragged back to the Midwest for an extended sentence.

After nine years in the laid-back, loose and casual wild West, life here pinched like a tight collar on a vacation sunburn.

Everything in Cincinnati seemed buttoned down or buttoned up. I half expected to see the bears at the zoo wearing Brooks Brothers suits, tie-clips and wingtips.

I felt like a coyote at the Westminster Kennel Club.

When people asked me how I liked Cincinnati — two or three times a week — I winced and joked that I was looking forward to becoming eligible for temporary citizenship in 30 years or so. And when I got lost — two or three times a week — I suspected that the street signs were deliberately removed from intersections to remind me I was not born here.

"Everybody's business is everybody's business in Cincinnati," I griped.

Now I like it here. No, strike that. I love it here.

Something happened. I don't know exactly when, but one day I woke up and discovered that my transplanted family had tunneled deep roots into the soil of Cincinnati. Maybe it was Reds games and museums, watching my kids thrive in a safe, exciting city, afternoons reading on the deck, listening to children playing in leafy backyards so green they make a desert dweller's eyes water.

Maybe it had something to do with the friendships that grow here, strong and sturdy, built to last by people who have their priorities in order: faith, family, friends and work as necessary. The Midwest is the glue that holds our country together, as different from the drifting West as tumbleweeds and oaks.

Maybe it was the thrill of coming into downtown each morning, descending from the suburban hills with the skyline rising out of the Ohio River valley like the city of Oz without the flying monkeys.

I have found mysteries and histories in those downtown streets. Red-brick relics from another time stand next to modern marvels of glass and steel, like square-rigged wooden clippers and frigates bobbing in a fleet of sleek cruise ships and aircraft carriers.

And on the sidewalks, the people smile. Some cities are bitter and cold. Some carry a grudge with both hands, or just don't care anymore. Some can't wait to bury their dead past.

Not Cincinnati. This town is laughing in the streets this summer at an elaborate practical joke on itself, mocking its own sober image with a tipsy litter of plastic pigs dressed like ballerinas, superheros, cartoons and porky swells in tuxedos.

The other day, Mrs. Helen Gripkey sent me a copy of an *Enquirer* section published on Cincinnati's sequicentennial, Oct. 12, 1938. The pages were sepia-brown, the color of memories, decomposed to a state somewhere between confetti and mulch, with a faint perfume of musty libraries and dusty antiques.

It was great. I don't remember Brucks beer, the Pike's Opera House fire, the courthouse riots, Ivorydale soap kettles the size of swimming pools, the Hotel Alms, Albers supermarkets, Beau Brummel Ties or Shillito's. I wasn't born yet, and I wasn't born here.

But sometimes when I walk around downtown, exploring old churches, museums and office buildings that could be both, I wish those were my memories too.

I can't think of a better compliment to a city.

"I need a vacation"

A spirit set free

Against a sky as deep and blue as a baby's wondering eyes, a flock of swallow-tailed birds challenged a wind that made flags snap salutes to the clouds. The little birds would beat against the wind a yard or two, then spread their wings and soar off like leaves in a hurricane, high over the big lake that was thrashing the shore as if the land had stolen the water's treasure.

I suppose a biologist would say the birds were just catching bugs, but there's so much of God's creation that cannot be measured by the cold slide-rule of science. Those birds were flying for the sheer joy of it. They were the spirit of summer, released from its winter cage.

My good friend Tim, whose diagnosis has taught him to measure one day at a time, has been teaching me to cherish and enjoy such small moments. We can't live in the moment all the time. But most of us miss them completely, consumed by the past and the future. We're travelers who watch the map and the mirrors, oblivious to the world we pass through.

That's what vacations are for — to float on the moment like a bobber. To let the past sink to the bottom and let the future tug when it's ready — not before. Otherwise, you miss the scenery.

The joy on a boy's face when his fishing pole bends like a question mark and he reels in a fat, yellow-silver perch from the deep blue darkness of Lake Michigan.

Cottonwood leaves whispering lovers' secrets to the breeze.

The crashing waves that rise and roll over the sandbars in Bahama-green curls, and hit you like a truckload of cold.

The hunched Michigan drivers who hurtle down the highways in a race against rust, trying to cross the finish line before their Chevy Coho or Dodge Dreadnaught rots off its road-salted rocker panels.

A lazy, sunburned afternoon spent gluing together a plastic model of a 1959 Corvette. Maybe it was the flame-decals, maybe it was the open glue, but dad and son were both 13 for a few hours.

I saw a ghost forest — the bleached bones of pines and oaks that had been buried by a sand dune on its restless retreat from the shore. They call them "blowouts," parabolic holes caused when fragile vegetation is disturbed, and the wind gouges a giant ice-cream scoop out of the dunes.

Some people bring back bumper-stickers from vacation that say "See Rock City." Some bring back T-shirts and hats. I bring home metaphors like the ghost forest, to remind me that a city is fragile, too, and ours is in a slow retreat, burying its own beauty under a harsh wind of bitter discontent.

I also bring back memories as warm as a beach in July: long walks with nothing but sun, sand and a knife-edge blue-on-blue horizon of water and sky. Time set apart, alone with the Author who wrote the story we call life, who knows the beginning and the end and all the chapters in between, down to each small moment when our spirit soars with joy like a swallow-tailed bird.

Mr. Mitty goes yachting

They call it the Scarab. I call it Scary. More horsepower than all the chariot races in the Roman Empire. A hull so long from its stiletto-pointed bow to the rakish transom that you'd need signal flags to take cocktail orders from the sunbathing bikinis on deck.

And it was on sale. Marked down. Must go. Only $257,000.

"I'll take it," I told the salesman at the marina. "Go ahead and hook it up to my minivan. It's the one with the lawn chairs tied to the top with frayed bungee cords and a "Clinton Happens" bumper sticker.

"Here, just put it on my Discover card. No? Any ATMs around here? Well, then, just bill me. That's Mr. Mitty, James Bond Mitty."

I must say, it was thrilling to race my new Scarab, "Missprint," across the sun-sparkled chop of Lake Michigan at speeds that are no longer street-legal, not even on Montana freeways. As I jammed the throttle forward, the bow lunged for the sky like a scalded salmon climbing Niagara Falls, knifing a shock-wave wake through air and water with a deafening turbine whine like the jet engines of a 747 in full reverse thrust as the landing wheels chirp on the runway and a cheerful voice announces, "We've just touched down, welcome to Reality. Please remain seated until your fantasy comes to a complete stop."

What was I thinking? Of course I didn't tell them to gas up the Scarab and hook it to my groaning minivan. I was on vacation out of state — not insane out of my mind. I'm not like those tycoons who fly around the country slashing budgets and adding links to newspaper chains so they can shower shameless wealth on major stockholders such as each other. Those guys could buy a whole carton of cigarette boats with their dividends. Not me. I'm just an ordinary, off-the-rack editorial writer.

So I bought the 42-foot racing sloop with the teak deck and deep blue hull and billowing red, white and blue spinnaker emblazoned with the clever nautical name I chose: "Blowhard."

I may not know much, but editorial writers know nothing if they don't know wind. I can inflate a minor misunderstanding with words like a bicycle pump on a toy balloon. Turning a puff of a breeze into a full gale is my job description. Hot air is my element.

So I joined the canvas navy, and stood on the pitched deck of "Blowhard" shouting commands like Captain Jack Aubrey sailing the HMS Surprise through a Patrick O'Brian novel: "Bend a sheet

24

to the fore topsail mizzen halyard on the larboard scuppers and reef the galley bilge," I roared over snapping sheets and crashing waves. I was not entirely certain what that meant, but as Jack Aubrey always says that Lord Nelson always said: "Just go at 'em."

The crew rolled the carronades to the gunports for a broadside, I waited for the rising swell and gave the command: "Fire at will!"

"Who's Will?" the cabin boy asked.

"Never mind," the First Mate replied, "your father is mumbling again. He always gets that poleaxed look around large boats we can't afford."

Mutiny!

Cast adrift like Captain Bligh in an 11-foot dinghy, no paddle, a dead motor, only the old Armstrong outboard. I paddled furiously with both cupped hands, cursing like a bosun until I finally struck shore, headed for the nearest marina, ogled the gleaming Scarab, inspected the racing sloop and then asked the nearest salesman:

"Can you repair a 1963, three-horsepower Evinrude outboard?"

I commanded his immediate attention. He looked at me with careful concentration, filing away details that would come in handy later when he gathered with his mates at the Tip-A-Few, to tell them the sea yarn about the sailor who walked in, soaked to his sunburned skin, wiped his brow with skinned knuckles, carefully appraised a 700-horsepower speedboat — and then asked about parts for an antique outboard that couldn't blend milkshakes at a soda fountain.

I hope he laughed so hard he broke a rib.

They say a boat is a hole in the water that you pour money into. If so, the Scarab makes a splash like the Titanic being baptized. My little 11-foot dinghy is an annoying drip from a stubborn, leaking faucet. A slow drip. Without a motor. No paddle. Up the creek.

But it has a mast and two sails. And when I'm at the helm, ducking to avoid the only part of a sailboat that is logically named after the sound it makes if you don't get out of the way in time (for lubbers, that be the "boom") — when the sails belly out like a fat man's T shirt, I'm Jack Aubrey on the deck of a square-rigged frigate, sailing into action.

That's what everyman dreams to be: Walter Mitty on vacation. "Fix bayonets! Stand by to board the Scarab!"

Spring break in Tucson

Horror stories about flying are as common as fleas on Osama. Since 9-11, scary headlines have made airports sound like the Bataan Death March with lost luggage.

It's not that bad.

The airlines may be too broke to serve those food-like substances anymore, but on our three-hour flight they generously gave each passenger several peanuts.

I was worried when they yanked me out of line and took my shoes, but they gave them back as soon as they found they couldn't sell used Kmart slip-ons.

And don't believe that stuff about "nobody is flying anymore." The line for the metal detectors stretched from Columbus to the outskirts of Delta, where fares are somewhat higher (multiply by 12 and add $700).

When our flight was overbooked, they offered a first-class ticket on Greyhound and free deluxe peanuts to anyone who would agree to be "bumped" before we took off. As we were pushing the airliner out to the runway to avoid exceeding our fuel ration, the co-pilot decided to take the offer, so it must have been a pretty good deal.

Yeah, I've seen the stories about people gnawing through their seat belts and attacking flight attendants with rolled-up SkyMall magazines. Maybe passengers are a bit more squirrelly these days. But how could you possibly tell?

Since Orville tried to elbow Wilbur out of the way at the Kitty Hawk baggage claim, people have been acting weird around airports. Normal, well-adjusted adults get within two miles of a departure gate and immediately get the darting-eyes and herky-jerky spastic look of a hamster injected with a Starbucks Big Gulp Turboccino.

I think it may have something to do with the innate human fear of being strapped into a sealed cigar tube for three hours with crying kids and guys who cough like Doc Holliday at the OK Corral.

This year, we planned our spring break in Tucson, which has Florida's sunshine without enough water for shark attacks. The Old Pueblo has been spreading like prickly pear since we left 10 years ago, but it still leads the nation in skin-puncturing plants, scary spiders, mountain views and guys named Chuey.

Its flavor is *carne seca* — spicy beef sunbaked as dry as a lizard's breath. Its colors are the bottomless blue of a cloudless sky and the dusty green of wild sage. The perfume is an intoxicating blend of orange blossoms and laurel. The desert's song is a warbling quail.

26

It's a coyote of a town, wild, shaggy, clever and adaptable to anything. It's not as safe as pedigreed Cincinnati. But it doesn't chase its tail and yap-yap-yap about race problems.

Blacks, whites and Hispanics have learned to coexist in the desert, making more than the sum of the parts. Cincinnati is still broadcasting in black and white, suspicious of anyone "different." We need a takeout order of Hispanic immigration.

"Put your seat backs in the upright position and remain seated until the plane comes to a complete stop," the flight attendant said as we landed. "And don't forget to pick up your baggage of race conflict," I thought.

"Welcome to Cincinnati."

Computer exorcist

Item: A new garbage disposal installed with adhesive tape that looks like the mummified plumbing in King Tut's tomb.

Cost: A maxed-out VISA card, two bad knees, mocking laughter, heavy cursing and skinned knuckles.

Value: Priceless.

Ask any guy. The real measure of a man is not sex appeal, annual income, stock portfolio or golf handicap. It's the courage to strap on a leather tool belt and go fearlessly into the unexplored frontier of home improvement. Nothing makes a man happier than to come back alive, dazed but undaunted by almost-lethal electric shocks and contusions, proud of wasting only an entire weekend to avoid a $25 service call.

Nothing sounds sweeter to me than the musical chime of ice cubes tinkling into my glass from the automatic ice-maker/dispenser I replaced in our refrigerator using "Easy to follow instructions" written in Portuguese. OK, so the icemaker has no door anymore, and the ice cubes eject like jet pilots whose plane is on fire. But I did it my way.

Victories like that make a guy feel like hanging out at a hardware store, swapping stories about rebuilt toilet valves and the mystical secrets of water softener installation. It's the kind of thing that separates real men from the "college boys" who will never live down the time they were sent for a tool and asked, "Where's Mr. Phillips and can I borrow his screwdriver?"

A man who can slay a furnace is king of his castle. But a man should also know his own limits. And I drew the chalkline at anything with a silicon-chip brain. That stuff is repair-proof. Just walking into one of those black-box superstores always made me feel like a caveman thawed in a microwave.

Computers and I have had an uneasy truce like the kind they keep tinkering with in the Middle East. Now and then I would get frustrated and throw rocks at my terrorist Macintosh, and it would fire back pictures of bombs with smoking fuses.

I knew about a place called the Internet, sort of the way the Bengals have heard of the playoffs. Can't get there from here. Not on my computer, which was slower and crankier than an HMO with sore feet.

But then one weekend I strapped on my tool belt, loaded my 50 cal. caulk gun and became... Computer Exorcist.

After years of muttering prayers, oaths and incantations over my demon-possessed relic, I replaced my rotten Apple with a PC Porsche: 900 megahertz of raw power. (For all I know a megahertz is a unit of pain, but I'm pretty sure 900 is about 800 times the computing capacity of my own brain.)

All that horsepower in my hands is like letting a beagle land an F-14 on the deck of a carrier — with his head out the window. But somehow, I launched my PC rocket into cyberspace. And now I'm thinking of moving there permanently.

Where else can you instantly find 3.2 million facts without stumbling on the one you went looking for?

Where else is there a staff of experts on call 24/7, ready to take your question after only 90 minutes on hold, so they can politely explain what a moron you are?

Where else can you destroy a whole universe — and restart?

Where else can you click and drag the Dixie Chicks into your car and make them sing in your CD player for weeks without attracting the attention of the FBI?

I used to think Napster was something you took on the couchster. Now I think MP3 is the greatest thing since the automatic ice dispenser.

I have not even begun to tap my new computer's enormous potential to make me feel like a complete imbecile.

I love it like a hammered thumb.

A fine idea gone wrong

April 1, 1992
TO: Amalgamated Widget Workers
FROM: Management

It has come to our attention that some employees want to participate in something called "Take Your Daughters To Work Day." Amalgamated Widget values families, including daughters, but human resources policy (Employee Handbook Section IV, part 17) prohibits the presence of unsupervised children in and around work stations, including but not limited to smelters, stampers, saws and high speed drills. Amalgamated is the nation's top widget manufacturing company, not a day-care center. Those who wish to introduce their daughters to exciting career opportunities assembling and packing widgets may sign up for the annual factory tour.

April 1, 1993
TO: Our Valued Employees
FROM: Management

Many of our valued Amalgamated employees were dissatisfied with our policy on Take Our Daughters to Work Day. After the protest work stoppage last year, Amalgamated has reconsidered and will welcome the opportunity to introduce daughters to the exciting world of Widget production. Smelters, stampers and other restricted equipment will be shut down for a one-hour tour.

April 1, 1994
TO: All Employee Persons
FROM: Management

After the successful Take Our Daughters to Work Day last year, human resources conducted workshops to explore possible gender bias in the event. Upon the recommendation of the Gender Equity Committee, Amalgamated this year will also welcome sons on Take Our Daughters and Sons to Work Day.

April 1, 1995
TO: Our Amalgamated Family
FROM: Management

The Gender Equity Committee has been expanded to include issues of age discrimination, after some employees protested that last year's Take Our Children to Work Day excluded grandparents.

30

Management has agreed to rename the event Take Our Children and Grandparents to Work Day — but that is not intended to exclude siblings, aunts, uncles, cousins and other relatives. Production will be shut down for two days to accommodate all visitors who wish to explore exciting careers at Amalgamated.

April 1, 1996
TO: Everybody
FROM: Management

The Committee on Gender, Diversity, Alternative Lifestyles, Age and Other Disorders has recommended the following changes: Childless orphans can bring anyone they want to Take Our Whatever to Work Day. For those lacking convenient neighbors or friends, human resources has made arrangements with the local homeless shelter to provide substitute companions. Also, parents are advised to keep their daughters and sons away from the cafeteria from 8-5, when employees who have ADA-certified alcoholism and drug disorders will gather for a keg party and limbo contest.

April 1, 1997
TO: Employee Pet Owners
FROM: Human Resources

A year-long study of the Amalgamated Employee Handbook has found no specific language regarding non-humans. After obtaining legal advice, Amalgamated will no longer exclude pets. . .

April 1, 1998
TO: All Whiners, Malcontents and Victims of Amalgamated Job Oppression
FROM: Former management

There will be no open house this year to allow daughters, sons, grandparents, neighbors, in-laws, homeless people, undocumented aliens, Internet-addicted exotic dancers, dogs, cats and tropical fish to explore exciting careers at Amalgamated Widget because WE HAVE NO MORE EXCITING CAREERS.

Repeated production losses in April left us unable to fill orders. Our competitor, Conglomerated Widget, has monopolized the market. All Amalgamated assets are being sold to pay liability awards from last year's event. The homeless man who was attacked by a Doberman belonging to our night foreman's alcoholic brother-in-law has settled for $11.4 million; we are still litigating an emotional trauma lawsuit on behalf of children who witnessed the unfortunate attack and the resulting limbo-party brawl.

Good news: The hamster missing since last year has been found — jammed in the gears of No. 1 Widget Stamper, which will not be repaired because the entire plant will close at the end of this week. To commemorate 79 years of Widget-making tradition, management has declared that Friday will be: Take Our Whole Famn Damly to the Unemployment Office Day.

Pizzas, ditches and summer jobs

"You just write that stuff to sell newspapers," someone will carp every now and then. No way. My first summer job was selling newspaper subscriptions, and I'd rather sell electric blankets in hell than peddle papers again.

I was 12, and door-to-door sales sounded like a better hustle than mowing lawns. "Make money, win free prizes, meet people," they said.

They didn't say: Make people angry, win free insults and meet large dogs named "Killer" and "Cujo."

I prayed every afternoon for rain, a plane crash on my house, a tropical disease — anything but another three hours of blistering heat, sore feet and the monotonous bleat of "No thanks." Slam!

I didn't learn as much as others who tell great stories about their summer jobs, but I learned something:

People with "No Peddlers" or "Beware of Dog" signs usually aren't kidding.

I could talk people into paying for something they didn't want, but I didn't enjoy it enough for a career in politics.

And if you want to sell someone a newspaper, skip the news, editorials and sports and cut to the clincher: "Color comics on Sunday."

The cold truth that more people read Marmaduke than my editorials is still strong medicine to relieve head swelling.

I learned a lot from other summer jobs, too.

The next summer I worked at an ice cream store and learned:

If the boss tells you to close the shades to keep the summer sun off flavors 15 through 31, do it or you will have 15 flavors of ice cream soup.

Working in an ice-cream shop sounds great — until you spend eight hours scooping, smelling and wearing blueberry cheesecake and licorice-ripple and can't stand to look at it, much less eat any. That's where your friends come in — for "free" ice cream.

Even more incredible than all the friends you make working in an ice cream store is what some bosses will ask you to do for a lousy dollar an hour.

Mine had me climb a rickety, bowlegged wooden ladder to paint a 30-foot cone. To comply with strict OSHA rules for worker safety, he told me to tie myself to the ladder with twine.

I decided I'd rather just hit the ground in one piece than get lynched on the way down.

I had another job parking cars at an expensive restaurant, where I learned that a Corvette is faster than a Jaguar XKE, that alleged grownups will do the dangdest things after a few dozen martinis, and that wealthy people don't get that way by throwing away whole quarters on tips.

At another job I had, I learned about the value of higher education. I was standing up to my shins in muddy water in pouring rain, digging a ditch with a "Texas teaspoon," when lightning struck.

Fortunately, it was the figurative kind of lightning that turns on figurative lightbulbs over your head. The idea that lit my dim bulb was: Hey, maybe all those teachers who told me "Do your homework or you will wind up digging ditches" were right. I saw the light and decided to go back to school so I could get a lifetime summer job for People Who Don't Do Their Homework: journalism.

I didn't make pizzas, sell hippie clothes, bus tables and work at other fatally boring jobs every summer while my friends were catching rays because I wanted thrills. I worked because it was a good way to buy shirts for school that weren't made out of leftovers from the sofa slipcover. (Sorry, Mom.)

But looking back, I learned a lot. And now I think you can tell more about people by the jobs they've slaved at with real working stiffs, than by any degrees from professors who understand work only in theory.

Manatees slathered in sunscreen

If this isn't heaven, I'm pretty sure I can see it from here — it's right across the channel on Boca Grande, one of the lushest islands of wealth in Florida, where old money stays in second or third homes, not rented condos, and floats on yachts, not boogie boards.

Hmmm. I guess I'm farther from heaven than I thought. But it only took me a day on the island to walk on water.

There I was, wading out into the surf when something large, tan and wavy undulated toward me like a family-size flapjack with eyes and a long, pointed tail, and quicker than I could yell "stingray!" — I walked on water back to the beach.

Well, actually, I didn't really walk across the water. That would be a miracle. The truth is I ran across the water.

What the heck, I needed another layer of sun-blocker anyway, so I would not turn vermilion and be mistaken for one of the Ohio manatees that litter Florida's beaches.

Ohio manatees are not the same as Florida manatees, which are so endangered they are only seen on license plates (which is just as well because they apparently resemble something squeezed out of a giant tube of ugly). Ohio manatees are not endangered. They're as common as Coppertone and smell like it, too. They're crimson on top, and golf-ball white on the sandy side. Only the shape is the same.

And just as stingrays migrate to Little Gasparilla Island, followed by hungry hammerhead sharks (why didn't anyone tell me this before I went into the water?), Ohio manatees migrate south each spring, followed by Michigan sand slugs, Wisconsin albino whales and other sun-seeking mammals from the Midwest.

The reason: Nothing cures a case of the winter gray-blues like a few hundred megawatts of full-strength Florida solar radiation. Even the EPA has not figured out how to regulate it yet. It's relatively free and temporarily legal — at least until the U.S. Surgeon General finds a way to stick a warning label on the surface of the sun.

And until President Al Gore outlaws automobiles, any ordinary American can change the weather. Just tie folding chairs and beach umbrellas to the top of a minivan, point it south on I-75 for about 1,000 miles, give or take a few states, adjust the speedometer to about 70, and you have instant summer in 16 hours.

My advice: Aim for an island. The smaller the better. The one I was on was so small it had only

34

three forms of transportation: walk, swim, or take a ferry back to the real world. I chose "none of the above," until I discovered that walking on waves did not qualify me to turn water into wine, and I was cast out of Eden to find a grocery store.

But that's the best part of island life: being surrounded by isolation.

There are people in the newspaper business who say they just can't resist picking up a newspaper on vacation. Not me. I can resist it without even lifting a finger. I can avoid watching TV with my eyes closed.

Accountants don't drive all the way to Florida adding up the numbers on license plates. Morticians don't measure every body on the beach. Lawyers don't issue restraining orders to their kids in the back seat. Plastic surgeons don't pick fights so they can rearrange someone's face.

So why should I care about the news? Millions of people go through their entire lives without a clue about what's going on. Why couldn't I survive a week?

I not only survived — I enjoyed it. No Monica, Paula, Carville or Clinton. No Newt, Arafat, Boris or playground snipers. The worst news I heard all week was, "It's time to go home."

And look what I missed: nearly nothing.

There was a plan to fix Social Security. A debate on race. Bickering about the riverfront. Big businesses got bigger. Chances of a tobacco settlement got smaller. Fighting erupted in the Mideast and peace broke out in Ireland — or was it the other way around? Taxes went up. Test scores went down. Ken Starr kept digging and Bill Clinton kept winking and shrugging.

When I came up for air — slowly, so I wouldn't get the news "bends" — I couldn't tell if I had lost a week or gained a life.

According to the Editorial Writer's Code, I'm supposed to issue the mandatory warning: What you don't know can hurt you, like stepping on some poisonous sea creature.

But I miss news-free paradise, where relaxing is as easy as surf on a sun-splashed beach; where headlines are treated like stingrays: "Leave them alone and they won't bother you."

A peace of summer

This is it, the weekend everyone has been waiting for, the return of my all-time favorite sequel that opens today in a backyard near you: Summertime.

The special effects are several warp speeds beyond Hollywood. Shimmering heat turns blacktop highways into mirage pools of water, that suddenly vanish as soon as you get close. Thunderstorms make the sky flash like a strobe light in a nightclub. The Ohio river slithers by like a languid serpent, changing moods from frog-pond green to sparkling gunmetal blue.

Memorial Day weekend is the first bell in a season that is one long playground recess.

The calendar says summer officially touches down in Cincinnati at 9:03 a.m. on June 21. But the calendar is uninformed. It can't hear the lazy bee-drone of lawnmowers, soft evening laughter on backyard decks, the sizzle of steaks on a grill or the splash and squeal of kids in a pool.

It can't smell oiled baseball gloves, cut grass, sun lotion, beech sand, blooming flowers, melting tar or the rumor of rain on a breeze that makes leaves huddle and turn their silvery backs to the gathering storm.

It can't see sunlight as thick as honey, white clouds like billowing sails or the intense, translucent colors of melting popsicles. A paper calendar can't feel cool grass under bare feet or the affectionate tickle of a hot wind through open car windows.

My favorite soundtrack for summertime is "All Day Music," "Low Rider," "Spill the Wine" and "Summer," by a mostly forgotten 1970s band called War.

In the bleak of middle March, I dropped off a set of 25-year-old Advent speakers to have them repaired, along with a museum piece we used to call a turntable. I had in mind a day — just such a day in May, with the windows open, sun streaming in and the antique stereo playing my skip-free album of War's Greatest Hits. Loudly.

And there it is, I'm transported back 25 years

"Driving round town with all the windows down. The eight-track playing all your favorite sounds."

The kids will interrupt "Dad, what's an eight track?"

I will try to describe an audio artifact from prehistoric times when the cuffs of my jeans were wider than the waist, before haircuts and shoes were invented, when college kids rioted to abolish the draft, not for another draft beer.

They won't believe any of it, of course. I wouldn't either.

"You had tapes that were bigger than my Walkman? No way. What did you carry them around in, a suitcase?"

Then they will want to know, "What was the draft?"

How does anyone explain that today?

The only war my children have ever known was the CNN miniseries called Desert Storm. It came and went faster than most movies. No reruns. You can't even find it at the video store.

But for the rest of this century, wars have swept through America like Old Testament plagues, carrying off and killing the promising young sons of generation after generation. There were only 23 years to recover from World War I before World War II exploded. Then five years until Korea. Eleven years after that, we waded into Vietnam for nine years of grief and grievances.

When I was growing up, the boys in my neighborhood all watched TV shows like Combat and Rat Patrol. We read Sgt. Rock comics and spent every waking moment of every summer day playing an endless game simply called "army." The rules: You were either an American G.I. or you were on the losing side. You hid in imaginary foxholes, threw dirt-clod grenades from imaginary bunkers, and when you were "shot" by imaginary bullets, you took your "deads" like a man — scoring extra points for dramatic head-first falls and writhing agony.

Here's some good news: We didn't grow up to be psychopathic killers because we played with guns.

And here's better news: Kids don't play war anymore. It's as forgotten as that 1970s band.

Unfortunately, so are all the American heroes who made sure the other team wound up losers. Thanks to them, we are at peace, and we have the luxury to forget what happens when we keep patching world trouble spots with tape, paste and appeasement, putting off the dirty work for someone else to do.

But sometimes a worry passes over like a cloud, and reminds me that "someone else" could be my son. Maybe we are like leaves in a breeze, turning our backs to the gathering storm.

But then the chill passes . . . summer's back, the sun is shining and we are blessed to be alive in a golden time, when children don't play army and war is just old music.

From caveman to Promise Keeper: Have faith

A list of lesser gods
we can control

"Right-wing fundamentalist Christians" are causing all the trouble in the world, a reader wrote in an e-mail the other day. Just eliminate religion altogether and the world would be a better place, he sermonized.

His understanding of religion is as thin as a communion wafer, but he's not alone. Many people are hostile to faith. And I think I know why.

They feel left out.

Once upon a time there was a god for every occasion and a temple for every god. Greeks and Romans could shop for designer gods that fit their desires like custom-tailored togas.

Then Christianity came along and ruined all that. Zeus was exposed as a low-voltage humbug. Neptune was a drip. Bacchus joined AA, Mercury is selling cars and Pan is peddling piccolos on the Home Shopping Network.

There's nothing left for the do-it-yourselfers who want to run their own universe with occasional help from little small-g gods.

I say if the federal government can hand out personalized license plates and surplus cheese, why not cheesy personalized gods?

What we need is a modern lineup of all-star gods. Such as:

Mercedes, the silver, 300 horse-power, fuel-injected god of material greed for all the people who are going nowhere in a hurry and flashing their lights if you don't get out of the way right now.

Cosmeticus, the wrinkle-free god of plastic surgery for aging baby-boomers who will pay any price for a 30-year-old face on a 50-year-old body.

Cyclops, the god of television, is already more popular than any church. Millions worship at his shrine for hours every day.

Laborius, a muscular god for slackers, works mainly to demand more pay and benefits for doing as little as possible. Every office has slugs who act like work is against their religion. Now they get their own god to prove it.

Faximus is the god of middle managers who sacrifice their marriages and families to their careers, foolishly hoping they will be rewarded in the afterlife by Mercedes. Faximus is the only god who has an office, but no real power to do anything without permission from his boss gods. And the other gods blame him for raising the co-pay on the dental plan.

Litigio, the smooth-talking god of crooked lawyers, can twist the truth so that right sounds wrong and wrong sounds right. Democrats often appeal to Litigio when they can't win elections (see Sen. Bob Torricelli, Al Gore, etc.).

Mediacrates (sounds like mediocrity) is the god of news. He can stretch trivial things until they appear to be huge, and make important things shrink out of sight. This god thinks he knows everything, and is a fierce defender of free speech as long as it is politically correct.

Pacifuss, the god of anti-war, is represented by a little clay protester with his head in the sand. Some of his most fanatic followers hate America so much they denounce their own country from an enemy capital, like Congressmen David "Baghdad" Bonior, D-Mich., and Jim "Jane Fonda" McDermott, D-Wash.

Pornocopia is a little pot-bellied god that looks like Larry Flynt. He's naked, but we're not supposed to blush. He is the second-favorite god of the entertainment industry, right behind Profitus, who can turn garbage into gold.

CAUTION: Commandment No. 1 from the Big God says, "Thou shalt have no other gods before me."

So use with caution. Little gods are manufactured for personal convenience only and are not intended to answer the big questions in life.

A letter to Screwtape

"I have no intention of explaining how the correspondence which I now offer to the public fell into my hands."

— **C.S. Lewis,** in his Preface to "The Screwtape Letters," a collection of letters between two of the devil's disciples, discussing their efforts on Earth.

FROM: Wormwood, Director U.S. operations

TO: Screwtape, Vice President Recruiting and Public Relations, Hell

Dear Uncle Screwtape:

I agree with your recent memo. It has now been 40 years since our letters fell into the hands of that annoying author and misguided philosopher C.S. Lewis. It should be safe now to resume regular reports. How lucky for us that his book was classified as "satire," entirely beyond the grasp of the vast majority of ordinary mortals.

By the way, did you know that a movie was made about C.S. Lewis? They called it *Shadowlands.* Don't worry, our friends in Hollywood turned it into a smarmy love story. His dangerously persuasive arguments for Christian faith were reduced to a subplot. Another victory for our side. Too bad we lost him to the other side. I'd like to see the look on his face.

So much has happened since 1959, I don't know where to start. The USA division is so busy we expanded from retail to wholesale recruiting.

We point with pride to a decline in church attendance and ending school prayers. But that indicator alone does not begin to represent the deep inroads we have made here on Earth on behalf of CEO Beelzebub, god of flies, prince of darkness.

For example, many churches are at worst neutral about our chief competitor's product (they are still peddling that old Gospel line). And some help us by updating hopelessly outdated Scripture. Remember those painful sermons about evil that we suffered through for centuries like heretics on Torquemada's rack?

They are sooo over. Modern Americans see no evil, hear no evil and speak no evil.

Example: The other day when some of our young recruits went into a Colorado high school and opened fire on students, killing 13 (your favorite number), not a single TV report used the word "evil." Instead, the killers were "good kids who made one bad mistake." Imagine that 40 years ago!

What progress.

That's just the latest evidence that our tireless efforts to turn the media into a neutral Switzerland in the Ultimate Battle have paid off beyond our lowest hopes. In many cases, the press is even our ally, demonizing religion and mocking the "Christian Right."

And we're no longer limited to the low-rent losers market with *Hustler* and *Playboy.* Some of our most effective sales brochures have respectable names like *Vanity Fair, People* and *Redbook,* which spread our message on the subtle scent of glossy, perfumed ads that trigger insatiable material lust, leaving readers feeling inadequate, empty and lost — prime candidates to reserve a spot in one of our hot new "eternal retirement communities."

Forty years ago, we were still licking our wounds from the loss of our star salesman Adolph. But we rebounded in 1973, when the Supreme Court legalized abortion. By substituting euphemisms such as "choice" and "rights" for harsh "extermination," we've managed to defend and even escalate the most brutal "procedures" of genocide. (I've enclosed a clipping of headlines from Cincinnati, about a baby that lived three hours after a partial-birth abortion. Forty years ago, something like that would have triggered protests. Today — just yawns.)

Our entertainment division is wickedly successful. We never could have predicted the effectiveness of steady doses of profanity, violence, crudity, nudity and anti-Christian bigotry. (Check out the computer games I've sent along, then pass them along to the Department of Agony and Suffering. They could use some fresh ideas.)

Our political division has set new standards that will make our job easier for years to come. As the recent impeachment demonstrated, the White House, part of the House and half the Senate are big buyers of our most reliable leading brands: lying and adultery.

In the coming year, we will be working with Global Hell on a much bigger scale. We've chosen the test market that has launched some of our most successful projects — the Balkans.

No matter who wins, we can't lose.

From caveman to Promise Keeper

Put 46,000 men in a stadium and you would expect to find:

At least 43,000 adjustable baseball caps that say things like "Valvoline," "Titleist" and "John Deere."

About 52,000 hands holding cups of beer. (Some guys use both hands).

Roughly a million profanities about sports, women, cars or empty beer cups.

Several fights.

Except for the "Your Message Here" hats, I found none of the above last weekend during Cincinnati's first Promise Keepers gathering at Cinergy Field.

No cursing, unless you count "hell," which sounded more like an exit ramp than an expletive.

No beer. Instead, all those hands reached out to grip other hands. And that explained the lack of fights, according to a cop who also works at Bengals games.

"No, not a single complaint," he said. "This is a very different crowd, very different. For one thing, they're not trying to outdrink the other guys.

"But," he added, "it's more than that." Yes, it was. A lot more.

On Friday night, falling rain and sinking temperatures couldn't hold down soaring faith and rising spirits. Late in the evening, every man in the stadium knelt together on cold, hard concrete to pray.

Nothing has brought that many men to their knees at once since the UK Wildcats lost the NCAA championship game.

"What is going on here?" I wondered.

Rob Becker had part of the answer. He was not at Promise Keepers, as far as I know. He's the one-man show, Defending The Caveman, that came through Cincinnati a few weeks ago.

His blend of comedy and science — sort of a humor-hypothesis — is that women evolved as gatherers, primitive shoppers who learned to share information by talking about how to find the best berries, what colors they come in and comparing the sales at McAlpin's and Lazarus.

While women were talking berries, men took off in hunting parties, silently focused on one mammoth at a time, communicating with grunts and hand signals like a modern poker game —

which is why we still can't choose pizza toppings during an NBA playoff game.

But rather than recognize these different traits, women have decided all men are a seven letter word that begins with "A," and it's not "acrobat." Our culture has reinforced the label by reducing us to slack-jawed simpletons in TV ads, whose highest goal in life is to run over something in a new pickup loaded with beer. Pop-cultural Man is an abuser of women, children, alcohol, tobacco, horsepower, pets, TV remotes, Bambi, pornography, credit cards, football, lottery tickets, insensitive jokes, guns, minorities, golf, power tools and third-world nations (this is a partial list).

At the end of his play, Mr. Becker yells, "Men are not acrobats!" — using that other seven-letter word.

Like every other man leaving the theater, I was sure he was right — about me. But after attending Promise Keepers, I'm sure he's right about thousands of other guys too. That doesn't mean there are not plenty of acrobats among us. But non-acrobatic men need to stand up like Rob Becker and shout, "Hey, we're different." Recovering acrobats should rise to their feet — or fall to their knees — to promise we can all do better.

I have to admit, writing about this is not easy. It takes more courage than an early tee time on Mother's Day.

Cavewoman: "How was the hunting party?"

Caveman: "We held hands. Hugged. Og cried."

Cavewoman: "Stop lying. You guys stopped at the cave of fermented mushrooms again, didn't you?"

In the news business, there's a technical term for groups like Promise Keepers: "rightwingreligiousnuts." They are in the same marry-your-cousin family with snake handlers who talk in tongues, twitch spastically and roll their eyes like slot-machine cherries.

Promise Keepers is presumed guilty of sexist bigotry because there are no women allowed. So women wonder: What are all those men talking about?

The answer is not new but it's true: "Not much." Or, as they said at Promise Keepers: "Not enough."

"Men need to talk about something deeper than football," one speaker said. Not psychobabble trash about being victims. We need to talk about being better husbands, fathers and brothers, who have the courage to stand in the gaps that divide families and divide men by our backgrounds and races. Amen.

Words can't describe the sound of 46,000 men raising their voices to the sky as the morning sun emerges from the clouds and floods a chilly stadium with light. But men who join hands and stand together to rise above a shallow culture of consumer gratification are one heckuva hunting party to find a better world.

Sidewalk saints

Bob Martina stands on a Clifton sidewalk three mornings a week from 7:30 to 10. But he's not pushing drugs. Quite the opposite. He's pushing life.

Although he might look like he's loitering, Mr. Martina is protesting — hoping and praying he can save a life by changing one mind of one woman who is on her way into an abortion clinic.

He was out there in the toe-numbing 12-degree cold on Wednesday morning, the 30th anniversary of the *Roe vs. Wade* Supreme Court decision that legalized abortion.

"I let them know there is free medical help if they wish," he says. But after eight years of passing out prayers and pamphlets, he has learned that success stories are as rare as miracles. "If numbers matter to you, you wouldn't do this."

His wife, Ginny, has another way of looking at it: "Mother Teresa said we're not called to be successful, we're called to be faithful."

Mr. Martina says he used to be fueled by anger, but now he runs mainly on faith, saving his disgust for the unconcerned citizens who have no opinion, who say we can't judge because exterminating human life is just a personal decision.

He has a special scorn for Christians in pulpits who waffle and wimp out, saying abortion is a private "choice."

"If Christians would have fought as hard as liberals did, we would not have abortion today," he says.

Mae Breadon is another Cincinnati "sidewalk saint" of the pro-life crusade. She started protesting in 1977, and has been leading prayer vigils and demonstrations ever since. Now 80, she has been jailed three times, including a 16-day stretch in Buffalo, N.Y.

On the second Saturday of each month, she leads a prayer march of up to 200 pro-lifers to the abortion clinic in Clifton.

"I started out by promising God that I would do everything I could to get rid of this," she says. And she aims to keep that promise.

Bob Martina and Mae Breadon are warriors in the spiritual battle against abortion. But they don't fit the media stereotype. "Everyone I have known are prayerful people who are just out to save babies," Mrs. Breadon said. "I don't believe in killing anything."

I used to wonder why anyone would bother protesting abortion. The nation is hopelessly divided. Abortion is enshrined as an entitlement — another sacred liberty stapled onto the Bill of Rights.

But that was before I had my own children, and saw their tiny hands on the ultrasound, and looked at abortion through the wide-angle lens, not just through my own myopic self-interest.

Now I can't figure out how anyone could NOT be passionate about it. It's the greatest moral issue of our time. And finally, it looks like the good guys are winning.

Polls show that people who call themselves "pro-life" are steadily increasing, especially among people under age 30, while the pro-abortion crowd is steadily shrinking. Abortions are declining as more teens embrace abstinence, and more pregnant women see ultrasound snapshots of the toes and fingers of their unborn child and realize a tiny beating heart is not a "lump of tissue."

A Gallup poll that has tracked opinions on abortion since 1975 shows that the number of people who think it should be legal under any circumstances peaked at 34 percent in 1992.

Maybe someday abortion on demand will look like another dead carp washed up by the high tide of low morals in the Me Generation.

"You have to be hopeful," Mrs. Breadon says. "Sometimes it's hard. But we know that because God always wins, we will win in the end."

Children of God or cousins of seaweed?

It all comes down to a bunch of kelp.

The answers to the debate between creation and evolution can be found in a tangled pile of soggy sea plants, snarled like Medusa's hair, wet and watery brown like weak tea, sprouting little gourd-shaped bladders that pop like bubble wrap when you step on them in the sand.

Usually, I just avoid the stuff like a pile of ocean yard clippings. But last weekend while I was walking the beach in San Diego, I noticed something new: Each pile of kelp contained a large rock. I looked closer and discovered that the rock was attached to the kelp by tiny roots like skeletal fingers, hanging on for dear life.

Eureka. That's how it anchors itself to the sea bottom, while the little bladders hold it vertical to catch rays of the diluted sun as it filters deep into the dark blue Pacific.

What incredible engineering in a lowly piece of sea trash.

In high school and college, I was taught that Mr. Kelp is my distant kin. We both evolved from the same "primordial ooze." Through trial and error, we finally hit on the right combination that opened the padlocked locker of life.

But I'm not a gullible student anymore, and I find that pretty hard to believe. It's like trying to believe that a jigsaw puzzle of Times Square was assembled perfectly by dropping it off the Empire State Building a few million times.

And here's something they didn't tell us in school: Evolution is just a theory. It cannot be tested and repeated. The fossil record that should support it does not exist. And the people who have deep doubts about being related to kelp, night crawlers and Howard Stern are not all religious fundamentalists. Some are respected scientists.

The late Nobel Prize winner Dr. George Wald, professor of microbiology at Harvard: "That leads us to only one other conclusion: that of supernatural creation. But we cannot accept that on philosophical grounds; therefore we choose to believe the impossible: that life arose spontaneously by chance."

Dr. Stephen J. Gould, Harvard professor of biology and geology: "One hundred and twenty years of fossil research (after Darwin), it has become abundantly clear that the fossil record will not confirm this part of Darwin's predictions. A species does not arise gradually by the gradual transformation of its ancestors."

That kind of talk was not allowed in public schools. Students had to be taught one theory only, the one postulated by Charles Darwin.

If students wanted to learn that Darwin himself said that life was "originally breathed by the Creator into a few forms or into one," they had to hear it from their parents. Or in church, like I did.

But education about the origin of life is finally evolving. The Ohio Board of Education voted on Oct. 15 to crack the door a sliver, and let the light of challenge shine down into classrooms.

New standards being adopted by Ohio would allow teachers and school districts "to include criticism of Darwinian theory as well as discussion of alternatives," according to the group that fought for the national breakthrough, Science Excellence for All Ohioans.

They call it "teaching the controversy." And there's plenty of controversy to teach.

The evolution-only purists sound like the Scopes Monkey Trial in reverse. This time, it's the education establishment that has its mind stapled shut.

Ohio made the right call.

I believe even a tangled pile of kelp is an amazing creation of God — but it's not my cousin.

Billy Graham's gentle rain

The rain fell gently like God's mercy on the crowd in Paul Brown Stadium on Thursday night. It was the opening night of Billy Graham's last Mission in Cincinnati. And the old preacher's power did not fail.

"Come," he said, as soft as the rain. And they came by the hundreds. Some limped, some slowly hobbled on canes. Others skipped as they clutched their parents' hands. Old couples made their way carefully as if they were walking on ice. Young families came down, wrapped like sandwiches in plastic rain ponchos. Groups of six or eight strolled out holding hands, arms draped around shoulders, bonded by the call, as soft as a velvet choir robe: "Come."

When I was a kid, I used to complain when those "gawd-awful" Billy Graham crusades moved in on my corner of TV-land for a week. I was mystified by the thousands who gathered in stadiums without a baseball game for an excuse. I thought they must be sheep on their way to be fleeced. Didn't they know Billy Graham was a punch-line for jokes on the *Tonight Show*?

I think the Bible says something about that: How God makes the wise guys of the world look foolish, and how fools think God's wisdom is a joke.

And now I know who the fool was.

On Thursday, I waited for the lightning and thunder to pass over and then sat with Dave Snowden, a pastor and Navy chaplain in the reserves, who drove down from Englewood, just north of Dayton.

We toweled the rain off our seats and listened to Anthony Munoz's strong testimony about his love of Christ. As golden sunlight made a renaissance painting out of thunderheads over Kentucky, the football hero said, "He has taken me to places I've never even dreamed of."

He was talking about his spiritual journey — a bigger adventure than the Super Bowl, believe it or not.

We listened to a host of angels singing from the end zone, a choir in bright red robes that rose and fell like a theater curtain.

We heard Michael W. Smith sing "Open the Eyes of my Heart, Lord," and a song about Old Glory that put a lump in your throat.

But the man who got the rock-star applause and whistles was the tall gentleman with the swept-back white hair. His topic was the story of the Good Samaritan, which he used to answer the question, "Who is my neighbor?"

"There are many people in Cincinnati who need to be picked up and cared for," the Rev. Mr. Graham said, "regardless of the color of their skin."

He spoke with power: "The devil is loose in the world today. All you have to do is turn on the TV."

He spoke with humility: "When I thought I was dying two years ago, my whole life passed before me — and I did not say, 'I'm a preacher.' I said, 'Oh, Lord, I'm a sinner — and I need your forgiveness.'"

And he spoke with love. His most powerful word was his gentle invitation to take the courageous first step and walk down to receive Christ.

"Come," he said. And they came.

And the rain fell like God's own grace, mingling with tears of joy.

Amazing grace

The human heart is only about the size of a doubled-up fist. But like a magical seashell that holds the sound of pounding surf, a single heart can contain an ocean of love that curls and crashes with the power and peace of green waves in the sunlight.

Most of us have seen the raging tempests of passion and purple storms of grief.

We know our love for our children and parents and brothers and sisters is deeper than the deepest blue Pacific.

But how many of us dare to leave our safe harbors and explore the distant shores beyond the horizon?

How many even risk losing sight of solid land — the friends and family we know?

How many venture out on the deep and let down our nets?

One day a friend of mine asked me if I would like to go on a voyage of faith. It was an adventure of the spirit, called The Walk to Emmaus, after the Bible story about the day the resurrected Christ joined two disciples on the road to Emmaus and revealed God's message to them.

Without knowing anything else, I accepted.

For three days, 30 men slept like prisoners on mattresses in tiny rooms at a former convent. We carried our cups from meal to meal. We were cut off from the outside world — no cell phones, pagers or calls. Our watches were taken away and there were no clocks. Cut adrift from time, we rose with the sun and slept when the "lights out" order came, long after dark.

And we loved it.

We loved the teaching about God's grace. We loved the singing that began as tangled saplings and grew into a chorus like a forest of oaks reaching for heaven.

We loved the hours in prayer and meditation.

Most of all, we loved God and each other.

Yes, that sounds strange. Women seem to know how to love each other without hang-ups and insecurities, but men use insults as the counterfeit coin of kindness. "Hey pinhead," we say, meaning, "I love you, buddy."

But through prayer, meditation and discussion, 30 pilgrims learned to love each other openly, without regard for background, jobs, age or race.

We arrived as strangers and left closer than friends, because we shared the "Amazing Grace" that a storm-tossed sailor sang about long ago.

The ancient Greeks called it "agape," meaning unqualified love. They had dozens of names for different types of love. Maybe our idea of love gets stretched out of shape because we have only a one-size-fits-all word.

I know this is an unusual thing to write about. Columns are supposed to be about politics, culture or Ken Griffey Jr.'s knee. The biggest questions in life are usually avoided like the weird guy on the corner holding a big yellow sign that says "Repent."

Don't worry. I'm not trying to argue for my faith as if it were as serious as baseball or politics. I just write this because I've returned from a voyage with good news:

Even oceans have shorelines — and they are all connected if we have the courage to trust God and cross a little bit of open sea to find out what's on the other side.

The heart can be a clenched fist. Or it can be an open hand raised to heaven, filled with so much of God's love that we just have to pass it on.

Mission statement

"As president of the United States, I, (Your Candidate's Name Here), promise to serve others with love, joy, peace, patience, kindness, goodness, faithfulness, gentleness and self-control."

Now wouldn't that be cool?

Wouldn't it be wonderful if our leaders hitched their hearts and souls to such uplifting goals, rather than panting after the shabby, fleeting rewards of personal ambition, ego and power?

Wouldn't it be fantastic to find a new Prozac, Zen philosophy or self-help guru diet that could make them — and all of us — think of others instead of me, me, me?

Good news. There is such a power. It's thousands of years old, but still works its mysterious miracles of inspiration and renewal for millions of people every day.

It's called Christianity.

That imaginary oath of office comes from the Bible: the fruit of the Holy Spirit, described by Paul (Galatians 5:22-23, one of my favorites lately).

Before your eyes roll out of your head and into the safely religion-free Sports section, let me testify that this is no sermon. I'm just trying to explain why faith has an important role in selecting our leaders; why Christians have every right and duty to squeeze and poke the presidential candidates as they shop for the fruit of the Spirit.

Americans have become squeamish about discussing religion. The media often treats it like some shameful social disease. Our culture is increasingly hostile toward faith.

Jesus said there would be days like these. The world is divided into light and darkness; those who dwell in darkness resent it when someone turns on a light that illuminates their ignorance and sin.

There's that word that makes anti-Christians break out in hives. Sin. Contrary to the tired stereotype, real Christians don't nag sinners to "Repent, For the End is Near." They seek a life of love, joy, peace, kindness . . . all the ingredients on the label of life. They try to lead others to Christ using words as a last resort, walking the walk, not talking the talk.

But there are times to speak up, too.

If other groups select candidates to protect the environment or a woman's right to choose, Christians have every right to support candidates who think the most important choice is choosing life over death. A good Christian such as Jimmy Carter doesn't always make a great president. But our greatest leaders — Lincoln, Washington — were men of deep Christian faith.

But now we are being told that politics must be sanitized of religion — something our founders would find very foolish and strange.

Democratic candidate Bill Bradley refused to answer any questions about his faith, saying it was private matter, off limits. Most of the media cheered.

Republican candidate John McCain insulted many Christians by calling the Christian right an "evil influence." Most of the media cheered even louder.

Both candidates lost in the Super Tuesday primaries for many reasons. But maybe voters are instinctively uneasy with someone who won't share his deepest beliefs with the people he hopes to lead. And there was no maybe about Mr. McCain: Voters strongly rejected his comments on religion.

Driving home from work one night, I heard a radio interview with a college professor who had a new concept: People desperately want moral leadership today, he said. They want to work for a company or organization that has a mission statement about doing the right thing, not because it is smart or profitable, but because it is ethical and moral.

Stop the presses. Mankind discovers the obvious again. The founders of our nation knew about moral leadership. Their mission statement said, "All men are endowed by their Creator with certain unalienable rights . . ."

That did for government what Martin Luther did for Christianity. To put it in terms the 401k generation can understand, we're all stockholders, not employees. And we all should seek leaders whose mission is ours, not their own, whose character is good, who serve others, not themselves. Faith should not be our only issue, but it is foolish to ignore it.

I don't know all the answers. I don't even know half of what I don't know. But the best mission statement is a life that blossoms with the fruit of the Spirit, and Christians should not be afraid to say so.

As Paul said, "Against these things, there is no law."

Tim finished strong

Anybody who met him on the street would probably think Tim Barker was just an ordinary guy.

He liked the ordinary-guy things. Loved to play golf. Loved his UC Bearcats basketball and loved his fraternity brothers from his days at UC, back when I was still in high school.

He even figured out a way to combine all three of these things into a golf outing for his fraternity, at which the main topic was UC basketball, of course.

I never played in one of those outings, but we did play golf once. It was the time of year when summer is just finishing the back nine and fall is on the first tee. I started out pretty good, then reverted to my usual hacking and slicing. Tim was just steady. He hardly paid attention to his own game, because he was so busy cheering for the rest of the foursome. The exact opposite of a club-thrower.

As I walked back to our cart on the fifth green, I saw him sitting there, turned a bit away, gripping his arm and clenching his teeth. Pain was raging through his body like a brush fire in a high wind. But he never complained.

I asked him if he wanted to bail out. "No," he said. "I'll be fine. Just give me a minute." And then he smiled.

Tim was on borrowed time, but he lived each day like he owned the calendar factory. In December of 2001, he was diagnosed with just about the worst news anyone can get: small-cell carcinoma. Spreading fast.

A lot of people just wilt and get ready to die when they hear news like that. Not Tim. He decided right away that he was going to fight. He didn't know how much time he would have, but he was going to make the most of every day, and the only way to do that was to stay positive. Have hope.

To Tim, feeling sorry for himself was just a foolish waste of precious time.

Tim and I met through a mutual friend, who knew Tim was looking for Answers. Not the kind a doctor or MRI could offer. He wanted the kind with a capital "A." Meaning of Life stuff.

I didn't have all the answers, but I knew where to look for them. We met nearly every Tuesday morning at the Frisch's Big Boy on Wards Corner Road. We talked about golf, friends, work, families and UC basketball, of course. But mostly we read the Gospel of John together, and tried to figure out what it meant. Imagine that. Two guys going deeper than power tools and sports.

It turned out that I was the student. And here's what I learned from Tim: Life is a gift, so treasure the moment. It's also a decision. You can decide to pity yourself and blame someone else when the clouds gather, or you can dance in the rain.

I learned that my problems were gimme putts compared to the deep bunkers of despair that other people face every day. Tim's hope lit up the world like a spring morning. His inspiring spirit kept fighting back to conquer pain, cancer, even fear of death. He found peace in faith, and hope that stretched far beyond the dark horizon.

The last time I heard from Tim, he was calling to apologize that he could not make it on Tuesday. He had just finished a treatment that had bought him 12 months last year, and he was sure his warranty had been extended for another year. "My doctor said he's never seen anyone live long enough to get two of these," he laughed.

A couple of weeks later, at the time of day when we would have been sitting over a cup of coffee and an open Bible at Big Boy, I got a call from his wife. Tim had died the day before.

He was just an ordinary guy. With a truly extraordinary heart.

The things we take for granted

Lessons from a boy's life

It was an April morning when springtime wobbled on its spindly legs like a newborn colt. The trees wore an uncertain pastel green, but the sun was strong and warm like a father's hug.

On my way out the door to work, I looked out the kitchen window and saw my 4-year-old son, sitting on his swingset alone. I put down my coffee and my important papers and went out the back door. To play.

"You'll be late," I thought. But then a little boy's smile beamed like a sunrise and I answered, "So what."

I can still see the breeze in his hair as I pushed him on the swing and we laughed and laughed. For some reason, it is tucked away safely between the pages of my memories, still fresh 10 years later. And I wonder: What have I put in there lately?

It's a good question.

The other day I got an e-mail from a reader who shared what he wrote for his father's funeral. It was beautiful, but now it's lost in my deleted files.

What I remember was how he turned simple moments into vivid treasures, like wild strawberries hidden in the grass.

There are moments when our lives are lit by love the way moonlight pours meaning and mystery into a landscape and makes your back yard look as exotic as Spain.

A good life is measured by how many we collect. Ray Neighbor of Milford knows this because he has what he jokingly calls "dead man walking cancer." The pancreatic kind.

"I just watched an excerpt from Larry King," he wrote. "He was interviewing this 8- or 9-year-old child with a terminal illness. He asked the boy if he was afraid of dying. The boy smiled and said, 'I'm not afraid of dying. It's just how I die that scares me.' Doesn't that sound familiar? I sat there in my chair — all 58 years of me. I am all that I have ever seen or felt. I am filled with life experiences. I have so many memories tucked away in my mind. I have a heart that bears the scars and blessings of many paths taken. I stared at the screen at this brave young boy who will probably not experience a first kiss; getting a base hit that wins the game for his team; crying alone in his room from a broken heart; staying up all night and watching the sunrise with his friends; the thrill of getting his driver's license; getting fired from a job; standing at the grave site of a loved one; giving the perfect gift at Christmas; being embarrassed in a crowd.

"I flat-out don't know what this life is all about. I do know that every now and then we witness

58

pure courage, pure innocence. We cannot escape the pure sadness of death, but within this sadness there is blended the breathtaking beauty of countless moments of pure joy."

"When watching this boy it took on a profound purpose. He made me realize that even life's hurt had value when faced with the reality of never being able to experience it. There is a deeply hidden treasure on this ride. We seldom think of it. We seldom see it until we see a young child who will be denied it. I love life. It is filled with lessons. Today's lesson taught by a young boy."

My mother wore combat boots

Contrary to popular belief, Mother's Day is not a conspiracy of Hallmark and FTD. It was invented by Julia Ward Howe and Anna Jarvis.

Two women. It figures. Men would forget.

Besides, men don't even talk about their mothers, much less set aside whole days to say thanks. If they are really successful and famous and suddenly have access to a nationwide TV sports audience, men will wave and say, "Hi, Mom." But that's about as far as it goes.

You just don't talk about your mother in public. And you never, ever talk about another guy's mother, unless you're just begging for free dental work.

"Su madre," "Yer mamma" — a sentence that begins that way in any language has only one way to go: Take it outside.

So you'd never hear me say something like, "My mother wears combat boots." But it's true.

Long before the Pentagon had a double Maalox Day at the mere idea of women in foxholes, long before the Navy got seasick at the thought of women parallel parking F-16's on aircraft carriers, my mother was marching off to battle.

She won the war. I have the prints of her combat boots on my backside to prove it.

She never actually smacked me that I can recall, but as a woman working alone to raise me and my two older sisters, she had plenty of opportunities for justifiable homicide.

Yes, I was the victim of what used to be called a "broken home." These days they call a divorced, fatherless family a TV sitcom. But when I was growing up, it was pretty rare, so people elbowed each other and sort of whispered, "Broken home, yaknow."

Other kids' parents would find out mine were divorced, and they'd give each other this look when they thought I wasn't watching. Sympathy. Poor kid. What a shame.

I'm here to tell you, they didn't know the half of it.

Now that I'm the dead-weight partner in a traditional, all-American two-parent family, I've finally discovered just what I was missing as a child: A chance to play one parent against the other and get away with murder.

Just try that with my Mom. She's only five-feet-nothing, but I'd rather have her on my side against the PLO, the IRS — even the FBI and the BATF.

She had to be mother and father to us all, and her father side never said, "Duhh, I don't care, go ask your Mom." Her father side sounded just like her mother side: "TheanswerisNObecauseIsaidso!"

And when one of us would get out of line just a little — say, leave my room looking like Pearl Harbor on December 8, smack a golf ball through the picture window or rewire the Hi-Fi as an electric guitar amp and play Jimi Hendrix feedback until even the neighbors' dogs howled for the cops — then the Mom side and the Dad side would team up like nitro and glycerine.

You could always tell when you were in for a pre-emptive strike of carpet bombing. There would be a small note waiting with breakfast. Just three little words we dreaded to see:

"This is WAR." The word "war" would be underlined a few hundred times.

Like massive stockpiles of deadly nuclear arms, just the presence of such a note was usually enough to head off Armageddon. Her declaration of war was enough to make me clean my room, mow the lawn, take out the trash, make my bed, pay for gas in the car, apologize to my sisters (gag), get a job and tell my hoodlum friends outside I ain't got time to take no ride — all before lunch.

Now that I'm a parent, I have to admire the technique. The way she managed to raise three kids without pushing any of us out of the car in Canada ranks somewhere between landing a man on the moon and beating Japan, Germany and Italy at the same time.

Thanks to the celebrated tag-team wrestling match between Dan The Man Quayle and Big Mouth Murphy Brown, we all know that Dads are an essential part of the family experience. Especially when it comes to carrying 260-pound coolers across a hot beach.

Dads are like the slaves who were crushed to death building the pyramids. They don't get a lot of credit, but they helped.

Moms are more like the Pharaohs who cracked the whip. And compared to raising kids, raising a pyramid is a cinch.

So on this Mother's Day, before I forget, I'd like to remind everyone that Moms aren't everything.

But they're close.

June 20, 1999

Fathers and kids

Most dads take care of their daughters like a borrowed Corvette.

You agonize over the slightest scratch. A serious dent could drive you to temporary insanity. And by the time you finally figure out how it all works, along comes some grinning wiseguy to drive off with her.

Sons are like a 4-wheel-drive farm pickup. You can't wear 'em out. They will go anywhere and do just about anything — haul loads of coolers and chairs to the beach, climb steep hills in mud. And when it's time to play, dings and scratches are no big deal.

Baby-boomer parents are too politically correct, gender-sensitive and bran-muffin brainwashed to say it out loud, but girls and boys are... different. We've been harangued by the equality cops to pretend pickups corner like Corvettes and Corvettes can plow snow like a Jeep. But no matter how hard you rub it in, no car-polish can make a 4x4 look like a sports car. And a Corvette is next to useless for hauling firewood.

I know because I have one of each — no, not the cars, I'm much luckier: I am blessed with a daughter and a son.

And I am a different Dad to each of them. Both are my favorite. And they are both, at the same time, God's most wonderful gift to me.

I guess that doesn't make sense unless you're a dad. But there is a lot of senseless behavior that seems perfectly rational to members of the fatherhood.

I'd rather miss the Reds winning a World Series than miss seeing one of my kids hit a single.

My 10-year-old boy beats me at Nintendo "NBA Slam Dunk" like Michael Jordon going one-on-one with a Sumo wrestler — and I love it.

The words, "Dad, can I mow the lawn?" are more thrilling than hearing, "Hello, I'm Ed McMahon from Publisher's Clearing House..."

I firmly believe peace will come to Kosovo, Belfast and Beirut before my two children last one hour in a car without renewed hostilities over "autonomous territory" in the backseat.

When I was a kid I swore a hundred times I would never speak the most annoying words in the history of parentkind since Abraham told Isaac, "This will hurt me more than it hurts you." But I can't stop myself from saying, "Because I said so."

Three airplanes circle a few inches below the ceiling in my son's room. The P-40 Curtis Warhawk is olive drab with big, hungry shark's teeth. The Cessna is cardinal red. A forsythia yellow

1930s racer is named after my golf game: "Mister Mulligan."

Each was painstakingly crafted during hundreds of hours of prolonged exposure to toxic inhalants.

Each frail little skeleton of feather-light balsa wood was covered with a skin of transparent tissue paper so thin it can be ripped by a sneeze two blocks away. Then it was sealed with thick paint named "dope" to remind you what kind of people do this.

These are not mere models — they are sculptures of machines that are eloquent poetry of grace, beauty and speed. The assembly method faithfully imitates the way the real airplanes were built from wood and fabric.

And one of these days, the boy will decide to see how they fly from a second-story window, probably with a firecracker attached to simulate enemy flak.

And that will be OK with me.

I did the same thing to the ones my father built for me. And he probably did the same thing to the ones his father built for him, and so on back to the days when cavemen and their sons huddled near a flickering fire, gluing flange A to spar C to assemble model rocks that were launched from a cliff.

More proof that fathers are irrational.

For years, they were so foolish they thought it would be silly to tell their own children how much they loved them. They thought the kids could figure it out by how hard they worked and the long hours they sacrificed away from the family, to give their children things they never had.

Now we know that 90 percent of fatherhood is just being there — with Nintendo games and credit cards.

We finally understand that our children are more important than jobs and meetings and the crisis of the week in Washington or at the office — but we still don't act that way. And sometimes we still think they know how much we love them without saying it.

The same guy who would never think of letting his 4X4 or Corvette run low on oil expects his kids to run on empty until one day they are grown and gone and all he has is a heart like an empty garage.

It's not so hard. Just say it.

Life is beautiful

We were driving home from basketball practice at the end of a busy day, and my son had an important question

"Heydad," he asked (that's one word), "what does liver taste like?"

That's not the kind of question I get at the office. Those kind I can usually field with a routine forehand or lazy backhand — "No, I'm not on drugs," or, "Yes, as a matter of fact I was kidding."

But how do you describe the flavor of liver?

"Well," I replied, "it might be the only thing that does not taste like chicken. And it doesn't taste like beef. I've never heard of a liverfish. So I guess there's only one thing liver tastes like . . ."

He could see it coming. At age 9, he already knows all the old man's moves. So he took a wild guess.

"More liver?"

Exactly.

That's what passes for comedy for the two of us. Pretty lame. Ordinary. Everyday stuff.

Like any two guys, we don't have a heckuva lot of "issues" to discuss. We just enjoy being together, at basketball practice, Cub Scout meetings, watching sports on TV, working on his Pinewood Derby racer.

It's the sort of stuff all parents try to sandwich into their overstuffed schedules. There are so many demands — church, volunteering, social events and work, work, work which can gnaw away at a lifetime of years like termites behind the walls of a house. One day it looks sturdy and permanent, the next day it crumbles in a pile of sawdust.

And at the end of it all, men and women who look back on their lives never say, "Gosh, I wish I had spent more time at the office."

What they miss is the fast-forward years of raising their kids, the magic island of time when separate, individual children and former-children called parents somehow combined to form something greater than the sum of the parts, a one-of-a-kind oasis of love and support, learning and discovery.

A family.

What we usually say at the end of it all is, "Gee, it went so fast. I wish I had spent more time with my family."

We realize too late that the really important moments were not the career promotion or the big presentation or the cars and furniture and houses we purchased and replaced like forgotten clothes in the attic. All that material stuff vanishes like footprints on a beach, washed away by relentless waves of time.

The really important moments are the everyday, ordinary things we take for granted. Just being together.

There's no meeting more important than discussing the day's events over dinner with your family. There's no deadline that is a higher priority than being there when your children need you, to share in their triumphs or hug them just as hard when they lose. There's no paycheck or bonus that can buy back precious moments we've lost. There's no job title more rewarding than "heydad."

Anyone who has loaded the whole famn damly in a minivan for a 10-hour road trip knows there is such a thing as being too close. But that's not a high risk in most double-income households.

Most of us are doing our best to prove we can make it without being close enough.

Most parents are stretched as tight as a hospital sheet, torn between the feverish temptations of the world and the responsibility and rewards of their family.

It's so easy to fall for the big lie, that the empty spot inside our hearts can be filled with cars, alcohol, sex or drugs. We all want to be loved, and our culture deceives us with a seductive Material World Mall overflowing with shabby substitutes that always leave us more empty than we were before.

If we are blessed, we learn soon enough that there is only one source of lasting, reliable and unshakeable love, and that the living, breathing, huggable expression of God's love is waiting for us, right at home.

There are some questions we cannot answer. Some things no words can describe. But this much we know: Life is a precious gift, filled with infinite beauty. It can be lost so fast. And we take it for granted every day.

June 23, 1996

If you're free, thank a veteran

In a drowsy little Arizona cowtown where fresh-picked cotton drifted in ditches like snow when it was 110 degrees in the shade, a mental patient got off a bus from the Rust Belt one afternoon and climbed a water tower down by the railroad tracks.

He threatened to jump. Said he was a Vietnam veteran. I told my boss about it back in the newsroom and he immediately offered to bring the guy down personally — with a deer rifle. It wasn't personal. Jim Garner (real name) just got ugly about that Vietnam post-traumatic-stress syndrome stuff that was a generic alibi for every liquor-store-holdup-hostage-taker in the 1980s. Jim didn't buy it. He was a Korean veteran.

I thought about Jim when I met Harry Falk, another Korean War vet who carries a grudge like a shoulder pack from the "Forgotten War."

"It's never been called a war," Mr. Falk said the other day, leaning back in his favorite swivel rocker as a storm outside did a convincing impression of mortar shells. "It's only been called a police action and a conflict," he said, making the names sound like four-letter words. "What it is was the Korean War. Everyone jumps from World War II to the Vietnamese War. They call that one a war, but if you ask a kid in school today about the Korean War, they say, "Where's that at?'"

Korean vets are always saying they were forgotten — and they are almost always right.

Next week is the anniversary of the beginning of the Korean War. The World Almanac says: "Over 60,000 North Korean troops invaded the South June 25, 1950." More than 53,000 Americans were killed (nearly as many as Vietnam in one-third the years), and 103,284 wounded.

Harry Falk can give you the numbers with exact change. He was there in November 1950 when 200,000 Chinese troops crossed the Yalu River.

His story is something.

Imagine being snatched out of high school and sent to Germany for the final reels of World War II; then shipped out to Korea for a "police action," armed with leftover weapons in a company of leftover soldiers, railroaded straight to the front to wait like bait for a human wave attack by what looked like half of China.

Mr. Falk was about six miles from the Yalu, where he watched the invaders cross at night on bridges hidden a foot below the surface of the water. "We kept telling our company they were coming across by the thousands. By the thousands. They wouldn't believe it."

He was quickly surrounded, captured, trapped between battle lines, then marched for eight days through nights that hit 35-below.

"The wounded, if he happened to fall back or drop out, we'd hear shots in the distance and we knew what happened."

Mr. Falk spent the rest of the war in a prison camp and was finally released on Aug. 23, 1953 — nearly a month after the armistice on July 27.

He still has the amber newspaper clips that trap his younger self in flashbulbs like a fossilized footprint from another age. His scrapbook contains the Western Union telegrams to his parents:

"Nov. 22, 1950 — The Secretary of the Army has asked me to express his deep regrets that your son has been missing in action . . . "

"Dec. 19, 1950 — A name believed to be that of your son is included on a list of prisoners supposed to be held by enemy forces . . . "

"Aug. 24, 1953 — Hi, Mom. Back on the right side of the bamboo curtain . . . Nothing wrong with me your cooking won't cure . . . "

Somewhere between "MIA" and "Hi, Mom," he remembers the chaplain who crawled through camp at night to feed wounded and starving prisoners with charred kernels of corn. He remembers the collaborators and turncoats and the brainwashing lectures about evil, rich capitalists, that sounded like rough drafts of speeches by Pat Buchanan.

"It was all about propaganda," he said.

Still is.

Guys like Harry and Jim remember because of all the friends who didn't come home. "Those guys should have some kind of recognition of what happened," Mr. Falk said.

They remember because a hot afternoon in the Arizona desert or a spring day on a tree-shaded street in Cincinnati is never very far from frostbitten Korean foxholes.

They remember because the rest of us forget. We forget that it took 42 years to get a Korean War memorial in Washington last year — long after the Vietnam Wall was dedicated.

And we forget that the Korean War is not finished. In a way, we are all like Harry Falk, prisoners of a forgotten war.

"It's still not over," he warned. "They're still sittin' over there on that line, the 38th Parallel. Sometime or another, it's going to happen again."

That's something to remember Tuesday — along with all the Korean vets like Jim and Harry, and the ones who never came home.

POWs can never forget

At the eleventh hour of the eleventh day of the eleventh month of 1996, it was cold. The wind cut through clothes, right to the bone, like winter's X-ray checking for weak spines.

I was standing outdoors at the Blue Ash Veterans Memorial Park, rubbing my numb nose, listening to flags popping and cracking like far-away gunfire. I had one foot in Korea and the other in Vietnam, studying paving bricks that are divided into our nation's wars, stamped like miniature headstones with the names of those who served.

Stars mean KIA — Killed In Action. Dots mean MIA — Missing In Action.

And I was thinking about going AWOL — walking discretely and quickly to my car to turn the heater on charbroil and see if I had any toes left.

But then I looked around at the kids: sixth graders from Edwin H. Greene Elementary, shivering in parkas, sweaters and paper-thin windbreakers.

And then I looked around at the veterans — mainly World War II guys, far side of 70 now, proudly saluting with bare hands, standing at attention in their VFW satin jackets, wearing those hats like opened envelopes, toughing it out.

"I remember a few years back when it was a lot worse than this," the speaker was saying. "Ten or 15 below zero and three feet of ice. That was the Battle of the Bulge . . . "

I decided to stay put.

So I stuck through the speakers who introduced the veterans chapters. Through the politicians who introduced themselves. Through the school children who read poems and placed wreaths at the bronze-booted feet of statues that stand for our wars, from Valley Forge to the Persian Gulf.

I stayed to hear the Post 69 Band put blue lips to freezing brass and play the Star Spangled Banner. And then at precisely 11, honoring the exact time of the armistice to end "The War to End All Wars" on Nov. 11, 1918, a white-haired firing squad shouldered 50-year-old Springfields and M-1s and gave an imprecise salute like a string of firecrackers.

And then the taps.

As the solo trumpet marched slowly up the scale, I could tell the bitter wind was making a lot of eyes water. Mine included.

At that moment, small groups gathered all over America to say prayers, salute and pay tribute to those who didn't return or came home inside flag-covered coffins.

And perhaps the saddest part of it all is that those who say thanks owe it the least — veterans who already know first-hand the high price of freedom — and there are fewer each year.

On most Veterans Days, those of us who have not served are too busy taking freedom for granted, working as usual or enjoying another routine banker's holiday. We should stop and listen. These veterans have amazing stories to tell, still fresh from the front-lines of history.

Lou Breitenbach was a flight engineer and top-turret gunner on a B-17 when his plane was shot down over Holland. He was hidden by the Dutch underground, then captured and held in a German prison camp. He still laughs at the "rumor" that someone caught and cooked a stray cat in the camp. "It was better than that horse meat the Germans gave us."

And he still gets angry at the movie "Memphis Belle" for dishonoring the men he served with.

If Mr. Breitenbach lived a real-life version of "Stalag 17," Louis Kolger's capture by the Japanese was "Bridge on the River Kwai."

"There was genocide by the Japanese," he says. "There was a holocaust. We just don't hear about it because the Japanese were smart. They didn't put people in ovens, they worked them to death."

Mr. Kolger was marched into the jungle to build a bridge. "It was the rainy season, and we had no shelter. The best we could do was sticks and palmetto leaves to cover our heads." Three hundred prisoners went in, less than 100 came out alive.

When he was sent back to Japan, he was loaded aboard a ship with 1,600 prisoners. "We were sunk twice," he recalls. Less than 300 survived.

These former POWs, along with my host, Korean War veteran Harry Falk, were given a special tribute at a luncheon following the park ceremony. They're a small chapter of a shrinking club.

They've stared into the gaunt face of starvation. "They'll eat anything," their wives agreed.

Sometimes they disconnect from reality. "Living with a former POW is not easy. At least that's what I've been told once or twice," Mr. Falk joked. Their wives seconded that one, too.

And sometimes they wonder why they lived when so many died. "I've thought about that many times," Mr. Kolger said, shaking his head. "Many times."

They wonder how they survived and about the guys who didn't — while most Americans hurry past the parades and ceremonies and don't wonder about any of it at all.

Now that's cold.

Letter to a graduate

The day was perfect as only the best of June days can be: a China-blue sky cushioned with pillowy white clouds riding on a gentle breeze that made emerald leaves sigh and wave.

I drove home from the hospital in a sleepless fog, brewed a cup of fresh-ground coffee and sat in the back yard, watching the clouds float by as it slowly dawned on me that I was a father. My daughter — that's you — would be a member of the Class of 2000, I thought. That seemed as distant as forever. It was as close as tomorrow.

Some fathers talk about the beauty of seeing their children born. Not me. I was paralyzed by awkwardness, feeling like the careless camper who caused a three-alarm forest fire, getting in the way while everyone tried to put it out.

For me, the beauty came later, alone in the backyard, looking at a perfect June sky over a world that was suddenly brighter, sharper, more focused and colorful.

I sometimes think it's amazing that your Class of 2000 has survived all the cultural claptrap and feminist foolishness and find-your-selfishness that we perpetrated on your generation. We believed boys and girls were just the same souls in different packages. We thought divorce was more healthy than two unhappy parents — so moms and dads dumped the misery on their children by splitting up. We were told over and over that day care was "good" for kids.

As I look back now to the day that we went off to work and turned our most precious possession over to a woman who answered an ad in the paper, who arrived in a rusted car full of fast-food wrappers, someone we had never met — I am heartsick.

But that's what "everybody" did, and somehow you survived it until the day came when your mother could be there to guide and help you when you came home from school.

As it turns out, your Class of 2000 is more mature by miles than I was at that age. If I had even bothered to think about it when I was a high school senior, I would have advised my freshman self, "Don't ride your motorcycle down the hall past the principal's office unless you are sure the paper he hands you at commencement will be a diploma and not a warrant."

My class motto would have been: "I feel like letting my freak flag fly."

You are less rebellious. More grounded in faith, more confident and poised, less squirrely about dating.

Yet you are also more naive about the darker side of the world. I sometimes worry that your generation's great strength — not judging others — is also your weakness: the failure to discern and, yes, discriminate between good and evil, right and wrong, good ideas and stupidity in a designer label. I pray you don't learn it the hard way as we did so many times.

As you know, I seldom write about family. But I hope you and others will forgive me my boasting today, as we forgive other parents who are so full of pride that they can't quite swallow and their eyes brim with joy.

You see, one June day almost 18 years ago, a pair of married children became parents, graduating into adulthood and becoming a family.

Exactly a year later, I sat in the same back yard and watched you reach for low-hanging blossoms and take your first, wobbly steps.

And now, in what seems like the same lifetime fraction of a minute, here you are taking your first faltering steps to the edge of the world, where you will soon fly away like a bird into the blue sky.

On graduation day, it is this Dad's prayer that you will have a life filled with the same love, joy and wonder that we felt on the day you were born.

Bonfire of the insanities

Introduction

By Heather MacDonald

The myths that control public debate about urban problems are not just wrong, they are dangerous. The notion that inner-city poverty is always the result of discrimination, never of behavior, results in policies that only exacerbate lawlessness and educational failure. For that reason, Peter Bronson's acid-sharp journalism should be required reading for public officials everywhere and for anyone who thinks he understands issues of race, poverty, and crime.

In April 2001, as three days of vicious rioting tore Cincinnati apart, the local and national media gleefully pounded out stories about the rioters' noble rage and the city's endemic racism. Peter Bronson was the only journalist to speak the truth: the riots were senseless violence, pure and simple. None of the justifications being so eagerly offered for the mayhem had any connection to reality, he argued.

Lack of opportunity for poor people? Well, if you drop out of high school, as do 70 percent of Cincinnati's inner city students, you can't expect to walk into a high-paying corporate job. A murderous police force? The police shooting that triggered the riots, Bronson pointed out, was a good faith mistake, not intentional "murder." A racist political structure? In fact, the City Council had spent years coddling black bigots who spewed out anti-Semitic and anti-white rants. Since then, Peter Bronson has continued to chronicle the consequences of scape-goating cops for urban problems not of their own making. After the riots, crime in Cincinnati shot through the roof. Hardly surprising.

The media and political elites had been telling the city's police that if they have "too many" law enforcement interactions with minorities, it is because they are racists, not because they are going where the crime is. The police got the message. Discretionary stops and arrests plummeted; homicides hit a 15-year high in 2002. Drug dealers once again control the streets in Over-the-Rhine and Avondale, because few officers are willing to risk the media firestorm that will break out if an arrested thug makes a "racial profiling" complaint.

It is imperative that Peter Bronson's fearless truth-telling reach a national audience. The political elites flatter themselves that they are furthering "civil rights" by attacking the police. Bronson explodes that delusion. Demoralize the police with specious charges of bigotry, he warns, and the victims will be the many law-abiding inner city residents who rightly see criminals as the real threat in their lives.

Nor does Bronson have any patience for the elite's anointing of race-baiters, such as Cincinnati's Damon Lynch III, as the sole authentic spokesmen for black America. Why not listen instead, he asks, to grass-roots truth-tellers — heroes like Tom Jones, "Babe" Baker, Michael Howard, and the Pastor Ed Gaines — who decry the glorification of racially-inspired violence?

The riots of 2001 do not set Cincinnati apart, though its well-meaning citizens fret constantly that they do. The riots could have happened anywhere, for the cringing deference to racial extremists that preceded them goes on in virtually every city across the country. Bronson's writing is the best antidote to that cowardice.

Cincinnati is lucky to have him, and now the rest of the country can learn from his wisdom as well.

Heather Mac Donald is a fellow at the Manhattan Institute and the author of *Are Cops Racist? How the War Against the Police Harms Black Americans* **(Ivan R. Dee 2003).**

The riots: Tell me about it

I missed the riots. Biggest story in Cincinnati history, they said, and I was on vacation. But I've heard plenty.

• I heard Mayor Charlie Luken say on Monday, "I'm completely convinced we're going to be a better city."

What else *can* a mayor say after days without sleep, listening to police radios doing a play-by-play of a city imploding? I hope he's right in the long run.

But for now, I don't think we're a better city. For now, it looks like we've become a lot worse. Scared. Angry. Divided. Discouraged. And deep-down certain there's nothing we can do to prevent an instant replay.

• I heard that a mob mentality seized the city. There's a herd mentality, too. Some folks are enjoying this. They think it ratifies their 1960s world view: White people are guilty. Blacks are victims. Cincinnati is racist. Cops are bad guys. The looters and protesters are right. And anyone who dares to object should sit down and shut up.

• I heard that the Rev. Damon Lynch III incited the riots along with council member Alicia Reece, lawyer Ken Lawson and some rhetorical arsonists on talk radio.

But then I heard that these same people who played with matches and started the fire are now "peacemakers" for calling 911 to put it out. Amazing.

• I heard a woman at the special council meeting on Tuesday. She called our elected leaders murderers, slave masters, official criminals of South Africa, Gestapo and KKK in disguise. Then, without a blush, she said, "If you look for the good in others you might see the good in yourself."

Unbelievable. Unless you have watched council meetings turned into bizarre circuses for more than a year by race-hustlers who spout vicious anti-Semitism and toxic racism. Some people warned it could get out of control. Council members said "no big deal" and did nothing.

• I heard about poverty. But I saw a poverty of education. A lost generation — the 70 percent who drop out of urban schools — is raging incoherently about their lack of opportunity and they blame the rest of us. Maybe they're right.

• I heard a lot about the black victims of police beanbags, but nothing about the white victims beaten during the riots.

• I heard about the "new Black Panthers," but they sound just like the old hate group that is no better than the Klan.

• I heard we should stop pointing fingers and move on. Tell it to former Safety Director Kent Ryan, who was fired to appease the mob as he was literally heartsick with chest pains.

• I heard that the shooting that started it all was a "murder," but it doesn't sound that way to me. It sounds like a scared cop made a mistake.

• I heard demands for "justice" — followed by threats that unless Officer Steve Roach is indicted, the riots will resume.

This doesn't sound like a better city to me.

A better city would say loud and clear that accountability is a two-way street, not a one-way, dead-end that stops at police headquarters.

A better city would thank all the good cops who laid their lives on the pencil-thin line between peace and mob violence. I didn't hear much of that.

On Thursday, I heard astronaut Charlie Duke tell 900 people at the annual Mayor's Prayer Breakfast what it was like to walk on the moon and look across space at the blue jewel of the Earth suspended in black velvet space. From that God's-eye view, the brotherhood of mankind is startlingly obvious, he said.

The Bible puts it another way: "Anyone who claims to be in the light but hates his brother is still in the darkness." — 1 John, 2:9

Don't shoot:
Are cops too careful?

This is an actual question from the 20th Anniversary Edition of Trivial Pursuit: "What Ohio city did NAACP president Kweisi Mfume call 'ground zero' in race relations in 2001?"

It's in the "News" category — but it's hardly news to any of us who live here. The answer: Cincinnati.

Here's a question I hope to see in a future edition of Trivial Pursuit: How long has it been since Cincinnati's "out of control" cops have shot someone?

Answer: 12 months and counting. The last time a Cincinnati cop fired his weapon at a person was Nov. 28, 2001. As Gomer Pyle might say, "Well, sooprise, sooprise."

For the past two years local protesters have spread propaganda that Cincinnati cops are murderers, rapists and racists. Boycott leaders who made excuses for rioters say the cops are "out of control."

But for almost 13 months, those cops have not fired a shot at anyone — while homicides are on a record pace and Cincinnati has more gangstas waving guns than a month of MTV rap videos. A bulletin board at First District police headquarters shows pictures of 147 guns — laser-sight pistols, sawed-off shotguns and semi-auto Uzis. All were seized this year on just one shift in one district.

So what's going on?

Some say the cops are being more careful, less trigger-happy. If that's true, the protesters should declare victory and turn their outrage on the black men who are shooting black men over drugs almost every week.

But some say the cops are being too careful. And that could be dangerous.

FOP President Roger Webster says police are less aggressive because they're afraid of being sued or accused of racial profiling. If they see a drug deal going down, they think, "If I get out on him, I will be a racial profiler," he said. "They're stopping to think more before they do it. They used to just jump out."

CPD spokesman Lt. Kurt Byrd says "de-policing" is over. The cops are doing their jobs, he says.

But Mr. Webster says morale is still poor because cops have no support from elected officials.

"They know there's support out there from the neighborhood groups," he said. "They want to do police work."

Last week, council heard from angry citizens whose neighborhoods are being wrecked by crime. And they voted unanimously for Jim Tarbell's resolution supporting the police.

But then a week later, they rejected a new contract for police supervisors. Given a choice between supporting cops or posturing for Issue 5, the post-riot reform to assert more political control over the CPD, the council chose posturing. Only Mr. Tarbell, Chris Monzel and Mayor Charlie Luken supported the cops' contract.

Mr. Webster predicts more "slowdowns" by angry cops.

One thing is obvious: Cincinnati's police are not "out of control."

But sooner or later, another bad guy will get shot by a cop. And then we will find out if law and order is back by popular demand — or just a trivial pursuit.

Ex-cop tells other side of beanbag shootings

After 19 months of twisting slowly in the wind, former Cincinnati Police Officer Eric Hall has lost his career, his kids' college fund and his faith in City Hall. But he has not lost hope that the city will still do the right thing.

Next week, the city will finally issue its internal report on what happened when six Cincinnati cops and two Ohio state troopers fired beanbags at protesters to clear an intersection on April 14, 2001. And it will be good news for the cops, said City Manager Valerie Lemmie.

"It is my understanding that they met the standards and guidelines at the time," she said. "I am certainly sympathetic to the concerns of the officers that this has been out there a very long time."

Lemmie said the cops are likely to be reimbursed for legal fees from the incident. "We will follow past practices and the contract," she said.

That's welcome news for Hall. But it's a bit late. "The city would rather bury you and call you a hero than support you in a controversial situation," said the former SWAT team sergeant.

He should know.

Since April 14, 2001, he has heard protesters and the press accuse the cops of a "drive-by" shooting into a crowd of peaceful protesters. He has waited patiently while promises by the city and police union were broken. He's been threatened with prison and $100,000 in legal fees, and warned that speaking up could be dangerous. But he's had enough. "How much can you take?" he asks.

By any measure, he has taken more than his share.

He was the cop who was injured in 1995 when he wrestled with Aiken High School student Pharon Crosby, on "Rodney King" videotape. Officer Hall still has a scar from torn ligaments in his shoulder.

That was his first look in the race mirror that distorts reality. Crosby was found guilty and had to pay an undisclosed settlement for Hall's injuries. But Hall, who is half Japanese and has dealt with bigotry all his life, was labeled the "racist white cop."

It was just a warm-up.

When the race riots erupted in April 2001, he worked 16-hour days, dodging rocks and a cinder block through the back window of his cruiser. Like other cops, he used non-lethal beanbag shotguns

79

on rioters and looters. He describes it as "three days of getting shot at, having (stuff) thrown at you, Molotov cocktails, putting out fires between fighting with people, helicopters, looters. I saw elderly white people who were pulled from their cars and beaten, young white kids who came down Vine all bloody and beaten."

Then on April 14, before the broken glass was swept away, Sgt. Hall was assigned to lead a Swat "field force," to protect the governor and other VIPs at the funeral of the young black man whose shooting by a cop triggered the riots.

They were ordered to clear a blocked intersection near the church, he said. "Our unit was specifically designed for that kind of situation, to respond rapidly, take care of it and get the heck outta there so you're not a target."

They ordered the crowd to disperse. But some protesters advanced, yelling obscenities, he said. One man stooped as if to pick up a rock, and the cops opened fire with 12-gauge shotguns that were loaded with inaccurate but non-lethal beanbags.

A woman from Louisville and two local girls were hit and injured. Hall said he would have called an ambulance if he had seen them. "I didn't see any women or any children. I scanned the area. There was nobody on the ground that needed attention. The intersection was cleared, so we left. I didn't think anything of it."

The "peaceful crowd" was not peaceful. The "drive-by" was a tactic approved by his supervisors, Hall said. "We were doing stuff like this all week. Why was this any different?"

The state troopers were quickly cleared. But the local cops were put on the rack of race politics. U.S. Department of Justice prosecutors threatened them with 23 years in prison unless they changed their testimony, Hall said.

"You almost have to entertain it to protect your family," he said. "But no, I decided I would not. I didn't do anything wrong. If I re-testified, then I would be lying."

None of the cops folded.

William Gustavson, a former Cincinnati safety director who represented another cop in the case, said the feds "wanted to convict some cops in Cincinnati to appease the community."

"I found their conduct very unsettling."

Hall ran up legal bills of $17,600. Then the feds dropped it. In December, the Halls finally received a letter from Assistant Attorney General Ralph Boyd, saying that "no federal prosecution should be initiated in this matter."

Publicly, the feds made excuses. But Gustavson says they had no case. The drive-by shooting by rogue cops was an exaggeration.

Hall retired last January with a post-traumatic stress disability. He says he just didn't care about his job anymore. He had severe chest pains and constant worries about losing his house and going to prison.

He is coaching, spending time with his kids and trying to start a new career at age 42. But he can't close the book on his last one.

"I am emotionally, financially and professionally fried," he said. "I deal with it every day."

The city paid $236,000, plus attorneys' fees, to the victims hit by beanbags. The cops are still waiting.

"I was just doing my job," Hall said. "Don't ask me to deal with the violence of your riots and not support me."

He may be the only one with the courage to talk. But he speaks for many cops.

Support your local police

When City Hall finally exonerated six Cincinnati cops in the "beanbag incident," one local TV station accompanied its story with videotape of a bleeding woman who was probably injured by rioters — not the cops.

It was an honest mistake. But it figures. The cops can't catch a break.

The scary story we've heard for 19 months: Six rogue cops did a "drive-by shooting" by firing beanbags into a small, peaceful crowd, without warning, as the city was returning to calm after the riots.

The report Wednesday was prepared by a Cincinnati Police Department captain, a lieutenant and four sergeants, based on interviews with 42 witnesses and 11 cops. It tells a very different story.

The incident at West Liberty and Elm streets on April 14, 2001, "occurred on the third day of a State of Emergency in the City of Cincinnati," the report says. The riots were just over. "The decisive action ... defused a situation which, if allowed to grow in magnitude, may have sparked more violence."

The crowd was not small or peaceful. Witnesses estimated that 60 to 100 people were at the intersection to protest during the funeral of a black suspect whose shooting by police triggered the riots.

The report reminds us what police had been through during the previous days: "Large crowds formed in the streets of the Over-the-Rhine and stopped traffic. Individuals in the crowds pulled drivers from their automobiles and assaulted and robbed the occupants ... (and) random acts of violence included one rape, 16 felonious assaults, including the shooting of a police officer, and three robberies."

The "rogue cops" were in fact the finest of Cincinnati's finest: SWAT cops who take extra training and psychological tests.

When they were ordered to clear the intersection, the cops "observed people in the crowd holding rocks, bottles and sticks." They saw members of the New Black Panther Party, who were believed to be armed. The crowd was loud, abusive and disorderly. Despite sirens, hand gestures and shouted warnings, the crowd refused to leave and some advanced on the cops.

"All officers believed the crowd's actions were intended to intimidate them or prevent them from taking any police action," says the report.

The police aimed at the most threatening protesters and opened fire. The crowd evaporated, and the cops left — following approved tactics.

Twenty beanbag rounds were fired. Four people were injured. A man was bruised and sought no treatment. Two children were bruised, and were treated and released. A woman from Louisville was treated and released, but later claimed more serious injuries and won a court settlement.

Too bad there's no court to "settle" the damage that the bogus "drive-by" story has done to our city and our police.

The six cops, who had to spend about $15,000 each to defend themselves, can now be paid back by the city. They deserve it. But Cincinnati owes them something else: an apology.

Aug. 04, 2002

Cincinnati's 'Bonfire of the Insanities'

Tom Wolfe, the modern Mark Twain of social satire, has written a book about Cincinnati. But even he didn't know the story he wrote in 1987 would fit Cincinnati in 2002 like one of his tailored ice-cream suits.

"Bonfire of the Vanities" tells the fictional story of a white guy who finds himself in the "war zone" of New York City and accidentally runs over a young black man — a rookie thug portrayed by the media as an "A" student.

Cynical politicians and white liberals pander to black protesters. A dysfunctional justice system drags the case out like water torture. The media sensationalizes the story. And protests, demands and threats of violence are orchestrated by "the Rev. Bacon," who shakes down scared white liberals with phony "programs for the people."

He calls it "an investment in steam control."

Familiar?

Change the names, make the white guy a cop, and it fits us like a straitjacket.

In Cincinnati, fact is crazier than fiction.

A few months ago, our local Rev. Bacons didn't wait for proof to demand the scalp of a white cop who was suspected of lying about his accidental shooting of a young black man. The reverends demanded a zero-tolerance policy on dishonest cops — and got it.

But now that a black assistant police chief has been accused of lying about damage to his city car, our Rev. Bacons say hold on — the suspension of Assistant Chief Ron Twitty (with pay) is unfair and racist.

Police Chief Tom Streicher is only enforcing the law he laid down months ago: "Dishonesty cannot and will not be tolerated in our organization," he said March 19. There was no exception for affirmative action.

And here's a plot twist Mr. Wolfe would enjoy: In response to rising demand to exterminate the drug plague that has infested poor neighborhoods since riots turned parts of Cincinnati into a "war zone," an undercover cop chased an ex-con who was buying drugs in Over-the-Rhine on July 25.

The suspect ran into the parking lot of the New Prospect Baptist Church, which is led by the man most likely to be cast as the Rev. Bacon, the Rev. Damon Lynch III.

An angry crowd gathered and was getting out of control. More cops arrived and later told Enquirer reporter Jane Prendergast that people in the crowd tried to punch and kick them.

The cops said they asked Pastor Lynch, who was standing nearby, to help disperse the crowd. Pastor Lynch did not return my call, but two of the cops who were there said he replied:

"That's not my job."

How's that for satire?

The funny part is that, thanks to the lawsuit filed by Pastor Lynch and others, that actually is his job. In the "historic" collaborative agreement, Pastor Lynch promised to work to improve police-community relations.

Instead, Pastor Lynch and his lawyer, Ken Lawson, are demanding that the undercover cop be suspended just like Assistant Chief Twitty. They claim the cops cursed and pushed an elderly black woman.

There ought to be a medical term for the mental illness that is making Cincinnati so irrational and delusional. "Bigot phobia," maybe, or "racial paranoia" — a condition that causes people to see everything through the distorted carnival mirror of race.

At the end of the movie version of "Bonfire of the Vanities," an angry judge tells the mob in his courtroom that the law is not something you can twist to fit your own warped opinions. "Justice is not a hustle," he says.

I think he was talking to Cincinnati.

Nov. 24, 2002

The hysteric collaborative agreement

What do you call an agreement that nobody agrees about? What do you call a lawsuit settlement that settles nothing? What do you call a plan for more accountability that gives the keys to our police department to lawyers in Washington?

City Hall calls it expensive. Embarrassing. A swamp of litigation infested with hungry alligators that charge $250 an hour to gnaw off your legs.

The "historic collaborative" to end racial profiling looks more like a hysteric confederation of shakedown artists.

City council members are having more second thoughts than a circus fat man on a trapeze. They were warned there's no net. But they shut their eyes and jumped anyway.

"There was a tidal wave of political correctness that swept over council, engulfing everyone in its path," said former councilman Phil Heimlich. "Our city attorneys, as was often the case, allowed themselves to be bullied by members of council into keeping quiet about the weakness of the case against the city."

Before he left council to win a seat as a Hamilton County commissioner, Mr. Heimlich raised stiletto-pointed questions about the deal. He was scolded by the mayor and other council members for being too divisive. He was told to sit down and be quiet.

Council was desperate to appease the rioters and the Black United Front. "The way the winds were blowing, whenever the Rev. Damon Lynch III walked in, he got what he wanted," Mr. Heimlich recalls.

The "settlement" did not settle a single racial profiling lawsuit. City lawyers still have to litigate those cases.

The city caved in to accusations of racial profiling that were never proved. The lead case was ridiculously flimsy.

City Hall surrendered to a class-action lawsuit that did not even meet the legal definitions of a class action.

It agreed to "collaborate" with parties whose idea of teamwork is to boycott the city, smear the police and tear up the "historic" agreement at City Hall.

Control over law enforcement was handed over to a federal judge. The judge gets to call the shots, the plaintiffs get to make demands — and the city gets to pay all the bills. What a deal.

Two years later, city taxpayers are paying millions to lawyers and consultants, with no visible results, while the city runs "Help Wanted" ads for a new babysitter to police the police.

As long as we're all laughing about it, I have a few nominations for a new million-dollar monitor:

Ohio Gov. Bob Taft, R-Vanilla. He never offends anyone.

If Gov. Taft declines, let's try his losing opponent, Tim Hagan. He's good at poking protesters in the chest and telling them they are full of barnyard bushwa.

Bob Huggins. Just the threat of having Hugs go off would encourage teamwork.

University of Cincinnati President Joseph Steger. If we're paying him $250,000 a year to retire, why not get our money's worth?

Ohio Supreme Court Justice Andy Douglas. The "Robed Marauder" who wrestled with another justice is just the guy to bring healing to Cincinnati. Suuuure.

Jimmy Carter. His Nobel Peace Prize-winning failures in the Middle East and North Korea are nothing compared to what he could do to Cincinnati. When he's done, the boycotters will have nuclear weapons.

The plaintiffs. Why don't we just give $1 million each to the ACLU and the Black United Front and send them to monitor Taliban prisoners in Cuba for a few years.

Now that's a good deal.

That's not profiling

If a dozen cops mistake you for a drug dealer, point guns at you and tell you to show your hands, do you: 1. Argue. 2. Act disruptive. 3. Speed-dial a lawyer to start a lawsuit.

Terry Horton and Vincent Clark chose all of the above. And now they're hoping to win a "racial profiling" lawsuit jackpot.

They have accused Cincinnati Police of racial profiling, illegal search, excessive force and illegally detaining them. They claimed that on Feb. 23, 2001, cops shoved a shotgun into Mr. Clark's face, searched and "ransacked" his green Yukon SUV and held them for 30 minutes.

The Office of Municipal Investigations tells a very different story.

There was no profiling. The green SUV was stopped because a bounty hunter told police it contained a wanted drug dealer. The SUV plates showed a warrant, and the man who left a downtown nightclub in the Yukon matched the bail-skipper. Profiling is a policy of stopping minorities at random, without cause. This case was not profiling.

• The SUV was not "ransacked." The report said it was searched — for weapons. That's smart police work in "high-risk" stops of dangerous suspects.

• The stop took about 20 minutes, and could have been shorter if Mr. Horton had not been "disruptive."

• The cops insisted that the nearest shotgun was 30 feet away. Officer Daniel Kreider was closest to Mr. Clark. "Officer Kreider was adamant that no shotguns were placed in the face of either the driver or Mr. Horton," the report said. "If anyone would have placed a shotgun in the face of either of these individuals, Officer Kreider would have been directly in the line-of-fire and he would have remembered the incident."

That makes sense. The behavior of Mr. Clark and Mr. Horton does not.

Mr. Clark alarmed the cops by putting his hands back in the SUV after he was ordered to hold them out the window. Mr. Horton argued and was "loudly talking on a cell phone while the police officers were giving orders to see his hands."

He was calling his lawyer, Ken Lawson.

Mr. Lawson has added Mr. Clark and Mr. Horton to 28 cases that were part of the city's collaborative agreement to prevent a class-action lawsuit over alleged racial profiling. The lead plaintiff in that class-action lawsuit was a driver who refused to stop when police tried to pull him over for a traffic violation. That's not profiling, either.

Police apologized and explained the mistake. Mr. Clark and Mr. Horton were checked out and released.

The cops said Mr. Clark seemed most upset to discover his license plate had an arrest warrant. The OMI report says he is co-owner of the SUV with another man.

Last week, Mr. Clark told City Council the OMI report was "full of lies and coverups."

Sgt. Brian Ibold, the supervisor on the scene, said, "This has been blown out of proportion to such an extent it's amazing. It had absolutely nothing to do with skin color."

Who is true or false: 10 cops — or two men who hope to hit the lawsuit lottery with a bogus claim of racial profiling?

The cops are not racists

I hate to admit it, but Heather MacDonald writes about Cincinnati better than just about everyone in Cincinnati. Her new book, *Are Cops Racist?* sees through our city like a 170-page CAT scan.

The book's message is summed up on the cover, next to a photo of a cop in shades: "How the War Against the Police Harms Black Americans."

That makes sense. Blacks disproportionately account for crime and crime victims. They suffer worst when the police are handcuffed.

"If the police are now to be accused of racism every time they go where the crime is, that's the end of public safety," MacDonald writes.

The New York City columnist and author has a way of distilling plain truth into Absolut logic, then pouring doubles on the rocks, right in front of the hatchet-swinging abolitionists of political correctness. A few shots:

• "For the past decade the press has been on a crusade to portray cops as brutal and racists, despised by the communities they are sworn to protect. That image is not just false, it is dangerous."

• "For the press, racial profiling became the very hallmark of policing, despite the fact that statistical evidence for such a practice is nonexistent."

• "As a cheap way to flaunt their own racial 'sensitivity,' politicians burdened departments with cumbersome and unneeded procedures to restrain police 'bias.'

"For in truth the anti-police campaign was a giant exercise in denial: It was a means by which the nation's elites avoided talking about the stubborn problems of inner-city culture — above all, its greatly elevated rates of criminal behavior." Sound familiar?

Law-abiding citizens, black and white, want tougher law enforcement "and have only contempt for anti-cop agitators," she says. I've found the same is true in Cincinnati.

But those voices are seldom heard. Instead, the people chosen by the media to speak for the "black community" are angry black "leaders" and race hustlers who claim looters are deep thinkers who are sending a "wake-up call" for more welfare spending.

In Chapter 4, "What Really Happened in Cincinnati," MacDonald writes: "The notion that this friendly, well-meaning town is denying employment to job-ready black men because of the color of their skin is ridiculous. To the contrary, Cincinnati's biggest corporations have long practiced affirmative action."

Her *City Journal* article about our April 2001 riots was passed hand-to-hand here like smuggled contraband.

The shoe still fits — and pinches some toes.

"The next time an urban riot hits, the best response is: do nothing," she writes. "Scurrying around with anti-racism task-forces and aid packages tells young kids: This is the way to get the world to notice you, this is power — destruction instead of staying in school, studying and accomplishing something lawful."

Good advice. Our Cincinnati Action Now commission has disappeared in a tar pit of "inclusion." CAN began with good intentions and swelled into an obese blob, smothered by its own "root causes."

But as MacDonald predicted, crime-infested local neighborhoods are now dialing a wake-up call you won't hear from CAN: "Stop blaming racism and back up the cops."

Hate crimes:
'I can see downtown is dying'

Al Sundberg tried to break up a fight on July 18 and became another victim of racial violence in downtown Cincinnati.

"I feel like I'm recovering pretty well, but I still have some places that are hurting," he said last week.

He was kicked and punched in the face and head by about seven young black men on Walnut Street near Mercer. He wound up in the hospital with a subdural hematoma and a cheek wound that became infected.

Mr. Sundberg was remodeling an abandoned building when a young boy stole a hammer. A co-worker gave chase and Mr. Sundberg followed.

"I tried to stop him from chasing a kid for a hammer," he said. He rounded a corner and saw his employee surrounded. "I thought I could take charge and use my foreman's voice. It didn't work."

Mr. Sundberg blames himself. "There were a lot of things I could have said better. It was a lot of guys standing around, looking for trouble — maybe selling drugs, maybe not. It probably didn't help that I was a white guy and they were all black.

"I don't know what was in their hearts when they started beating on me."

Mona C. is afraid she will get in trouble for saying she was harassed because she is white.

She and her husband were downtown on a Sunday afternoon when a group of black kids started throwing wadded up paper at them as they walked north on Vine Street near Fountain Square. They called 911.

She said a cop told her, "They're just angry all the time and it doesn't do much good to press charges because they will get off anyway."

Paula Dickerson was leaving the Riverfest fireworks on Labor Day weekend when roadblocks detoured her to Vine Street.

Her SUV was stuck in traffic with the top down when, "I saw this thing go whipping past my eye. It was an egg. They were hitting the inside of the vehicle and hitting us."

The eggs were followed by bottles. Some of the young men were screaming "cracker," "white hillbillies" and "white b——," she said. The frightened girls in her car suffered cuts on their arms and legs. "The crowd was male and female, from 8 years old to an older gentleman of about 60, who said, 'What do you expect coming down here?' "

Ms. Dickerson of Mason is a junior at Wright State in Dayton. "I love Cincinnati. It won't keep me from going downtown," she said.

Mr. Sundberg still works downtown, but his men leave the job in pairs now. "He doesn't like to go downtown anymore," said his wife, Terri.

Mona C. is more blunt. "Now I see ads saying 'C'mon downtown' and I say, 'Yeah, sure.' I can see downtown dying."

Police are shifting downtown foot-patrol manpower to the evening hours to control large crowds of youths who gather there after school.

Downtown is still safe. This stuff is rare. But not rare enough. If whites treated blacks this way, we'd call it "hate crime."

This weekend was the best of downtown. These victims saw the worst.

April 28, 2002

Hell Town:
Good people try not to get shot

The sidewalks are paved with sparkling glass, and young men carry bright green bouquets of fresh cash. Nobody seems to work here, but it's not paradise.

A better name for this slice of Cincinnati is spray-painted on weathered plywood: "Hell Town," it says on a derelict building.

It's the poorest, most dangerous part of Over-the-Rhine — from Central Parkway on the west to Vine Street on the east, from Washington Park at the bottom to Findlay Market at the top. It has streets named Pleasant and Race and an alley at 13th and Republic that police say is one of the most hazardous spots in Cincinnati.

This is where a cop shot a black man who was running from police and ... well, we all know that story.

This is also a part of town where good people try to get by without getting shot.

An elderly man in a barbershop sums it up: "We all want the same thing — good schools and a safe place for our children to play. We want jobs."

Well, some want jobs. Not the drug boys who hang on the corners like clusters of poison grapes. They already have a "job," running a drive-through for dopers: OxyContin, pot, coke, smack and soul-stealing crack.

White kids from the suburbs sit in mommy's SUV and place their orders. A girl of about 16 had the scared and excited look of a kid at Paramount's Kings Island, but she and her apparent boyfriend with the styled white-boy dreadlocks were looking for another kind of thrill ride.

They are safe, if they stay in the car. After all, they're trade partners for Hell Town's leading export.

Mixed in with the white kids' Chevy Blazers are the polished Jaguars and gold-jeweled Caddys of the drug bosses, who float by like the biggest fish in the tank.

"Urban Taliban," says my friend and guide, Michael Howard, shaking his head as he passes out fliers for Mount Auburn United Methodist Church. On the street he is "Nitty," from his days as a boxer, enforcer, addict and thief who did two tours of Ohio prisons. Now he spreads the gospel of Christ and the American dream, his "keys to hope for the hopeless."

94

He has no respect for the reverends who show up only for protest marches. "I'm boycotting too," he says. "I'm boycotting the cycle of poverty, drugs, domestic violence, poor education, economic exclusion — anything that stands in the way of the American dream."

The drug boys take the fliers. They look at me suspiciously, probably the way people in white neighborhoods look at them. Two kinds of white people are safe here, I'm told: drug customers, and Christians who come to help.

Nobody is safe at night.

Bullet-pocked bricks mark a drive-by shooting that was never reported. No big deal — they missed. Businesses cling to Vine Street, slowly dying like frost-burned thistles in an abandoned garden.

Old guys stumble by with eyes the color of watery custard — husks of drug boys. Prison and abuse have made them thin as a bum's socks.

Mike breaks up an argument that is climbing into the high notes where words give out and gunshots take over. A girl who should be in school watches while her tiny baby peeks out from blankets in a buggy, wide-eyed and innocent. This is the face of Cincinnati's future.

God help the child. Who else will?

Vine Street:
What was the excuse this time?

There was no police shooting, no reverends shouting for justice this time — just 300 black people blocking Vine Street on Monday night, pelting cars with rocks, bottles and eggs and yelling "get whitey."

Some cities would call that a riot. Cincinnati didn't even call it a "disturbance." The headline over a 3-inch story in the *Enquirer* the next day said, "Fight draws crowd; police close street."

Witnesses and police reports showed something worse: frightening attacks on cars driven by white people, while cars driven by blacks were waved through.

Police said it started when two girls, ages 14 and 17, started throwing punches in the street. As cops arrested the girls, the 14-year-old struggled and spit in the face of one officer. The 17-year-old's brother, 12, jumped on a cop — and it took two more to restrain him.

The crowd swelled to 300, and 20 to 50 people began throwing things. The cops backed off to regroup.

Police logs show several calls from trapped motorists.

"Group of male black suspects threw rocks, eggs at his car; yelled things about his being white," says one dispatcher's report.

"They were running up and throwing things at the windows of cars and yelling, 'Get whitey,'" said a woman who did not want to be named because she lives nearby and fears reprisals.

University of Cincinnati student Steve Wahoff was caught in the middle of it. "I was giving a buddy a ride downtown. Vine is the quickest route. I knew it was sort of dangerous. But it was still light out, so I thought there would be no problem," he said. "I saw this large crowd in the street and thought, 'I'd better get out of here.' And right then, this huge rock hit the windshield."

As he hit the gas and fled, he noticed that black motorists were not bothered at all, and one tried to block his escape. Damage estimates for his car were $800, not including a windshield replacement, he said. "That's the last time I go down Vine Street."

Kiril Merjanski, a Bulgarian writer and poet who has been in the United States just three months, was also caught in the mob with his wife. "We were really scared," he said. "Things are not good in Bulgaria, but this type of thing would never happen there."

Their car was hit with eggs and rocks, causing about $1,000 in damage, according to police reports.

Michael Howard, an outreach coordinator for Mount Auburn Methodist Church, was walking on Vine Street. "There's an element down there that is growing in disrespect for the law," he said.

Mr. Howard, who is black, says Cincinnati is reluctant to face what happened because "we don't want to return to the riots of last April."

"But a lot of people are going to be hurt and a lot of property is going to be damaged if we don't take control."

So what's the excuse? What's the politically correct "root cause" for racial violence that makes Cincinnati look worse than Bulgaria?

"I don't know about all this," Mr. Merjanski said. "I don't know what the problem is."

Nobody does.

'Put the razor-wire back in our laws'

Knock, knock. Mason, Indian Hill, Hyde Park and Hamilton, are you home? Hello? Hello? Milford, Montgomery, Fairfield, Delhi, West Chester, Anderson and Cheviot, are you listening?

Cincinnati is in trouble. And this is what it looks like.

"Everywhere you looked, drugs were being sold. Every drug imaginable."

"There were as many as 25 young men in one location. They're dangerous and confrontational. There's fighting, shootings and sometimes murder. The residents are often terrified of crossing the dealers' boundaries and won't let their children play outside."

"They told my 10-year old daughter, `We're gonna kill your dog.'"

"My son bought drugs from them. He died of a heroin overdose."

"I watched the young men get into cars and then get out with fistfuls of money."

"I see them on the corner at 6 a.m. and at 10 p.m. They wake me up at 2 a.m. with profanity. I see a hundred drug deals a day."

These are cries for help from ordinary people who are watching drug-crime cancer kill their neighborhoods. They came from Northside, Madisonville, Walnut Hills, Bond Hill, Mount Auburn, Over-the-Rhine, Mount Washington and College Hill — some of Cincinnati's oldest neighborhoods.

They lined up to tell their stories at a Dec. 10 Law and Public Safety Committee hearing on a loitering ordinance to help bust pushers. For hours, they vented pain, frustration, grief, fear and disbelief that their peaceful world has been invaded. Emotions were drawn bowstring tight with anger. Voices shook with tears of frustration and despair.

Gina Strohm brought along bullets she dug out of a building her family owns. "I am appalled at the inaction," she said.

Bob Pickford of Findlay Market told about a man who was beaten to death in the middle of the street at 11 a.m., "in full view of the market and our customers."

Hal McKinney of Northside said property values are sinking like homeowners' hopes. One house dropped from $90,000 to $43,000. Another fell from $80,000 to $30,000. "Crack rats" have shot at him and threatened to torch his home. "Two years ago, I was one of those people who didn't care," he says. "I had no concept."

Amos Robinson of College Hill wants someone to stop the young "drug boys in training," who work for dealers running cash and crack.

Taylor Jameson is ready to give up on her hair salon in Northside. "There's no escape. I'm fighting for my life and my rights to lead a happy, normal life."

Sharon Koehler of Northside said a backlash against "criminals and terrorists" has been simmering for a long time. "It has to stop. I refuse to back down. It's high time we put the razor wire back into our laws. Take the handcuffs off the police and put them back on the criminals."

City Hall is finally getting a clue. Maybe. The cops are ramping up their drug busts, the mayor wants tougher sentencing and some council members are talking tough about crime after two years of politically correct pandering to protesters. For nearly two years, the city has responded to riots and lawlessness not with law and order, but by blaming the cops. Our city was held hostage to a handful of activists who cried "racism" to excuse criminals — and we reaped a record harvest of corpses and crime.

If Cincinnati is waking up, Dec. 10 was the alarm clock. But the battle is just beginning. And it's not just for Northside or Madisonville. This is everyone's fight to save the city — or there will be nobody home when it's your turn to call for help.

Boycott this

When the U.S. troops get done fumigating Saddam's palaces, maybe they can come home and liberate Cincinnati. They'd find that the scenery looks very familiar.

We have our own United Nations "collaborative" that does nothing but talk and delay and undermine the police troops who are trying to protect us.

We have a Hans Blix federal monitor who has to keep looking for problems or he's out of a job. So far, the city and the police have adopted dozens of reforms to comply with toothless U.N. collaborative resolutions. The defiant Iraq plaintiffs have done nothing. But whom did the monitor blast? The city and the cops, of course.

We have protesters who think they can get peace by breaking windows, and appeasers who cater to demands from boycott dictators the way Germany fills Saddam's orders for gas masks.

We even have a federal judge who acts like France. She sides with the boycotters who threaten our city, and blasts our elected City Council members for daring to criticize them.

The boycotters' demands change like the flavor of the week. Maybe it's time for a list of demands to *them* for a change.

Such as:

• Stop spouting anti-Semitic and racist mustard gas and publicly condemn the people who do.

• Show us your membership. Federal Judge Susan Dlott doesn't seem to think it's important. But when you make demands for $1.5 billion in "programs," we have a right to know who's asking.

• Do something to reduce the number of teen pregnancies that aggravate poverty and school dropouts, which are far bigger obstacles than exaggerated racism.

• Teach young people not to run, fight or lie when they are confronted by a cop.

• Help the police clean up crime by reporting it. Stop pretending nobody saw drug deals, beatings and murders in front of 20 witnesses.

• Speak up about black-on-black violence and killings, which are a far greater health hazard than collateral damage from a cop.

• Condemn hate crimes and violence, rioting, looting and assaults on innocent whites.

• Recognize that protests and boycotts have consequences, and take responsibility for lost jobs and economic hardship on people who can least afford it.

• If you want to talk the talk of moral leadership, start walking the walk. Church leaders who fail to condemn people who bear false witness against our city and our police are hypocrites. Community leaders who stand by and say nothing are wimps.

• Boycott drugs and crime that are killing our neighborhoods.

I suppose some people will say this list of demands is "unreasonable." No problem. It can be amended daily to refine it from "unreasonable" to "totally ludicrous."

Besides, why should only one side be allowed to make ridiculous, divisive demands?

I say it's my way or the highway to Baghdad on the Ohio River.

Politically incorrect —
and proud of it

A victim of campus ridicule

Critics say the French film *Ridicule* is "handsome, ravishing, witty, intelligent and quintessentially French."

"It's a very successful and respected film taught in a lot of French departments," said Jonathan Strauss, chairman of Miami University's French and Italian department.

But Miami student Aaron Sanders says some students think *Ridicule* looks more like a French postcard. In his column in the *Miami Student*, he said showing it in a French class was "bordering on pure pornography."

Now Sanders has been "terminated" as a columnist.

What most critics don't say is that *Ridicule* opens like a zipper, with a graphic close-up of a man urinating on another man's head. The only review I found that even mentioned the scene said, "There it is, big as day, a penis on screen."

Handsome. Ravishing.

OK, so it's a matter of opinion. But so was Sanders' column. He described the movie, quoting unidentified students who watched it in Claire Goldstein's French class, "Text in Context." The students didn't want to be quoted and risk a bad grade, Sanders said, but some were deeply offended.

"Time and again, professors will try to pass along nonsense for what they believe is education," he wrote on Jan. 17 under the headline "Hold MU professors accountable." He said Strauss also "consistently subjects (students) to books and films that contain lewd, sexual content, rape and incest — many seemingly condoning it."

Le merde hit le fan. Strauss protested to the *Miami Student* faculty adviser, journalism professor Cheryl Heckler. "We both agreed it was incredibly irresponsible reporting," Heckler said.

Heckler wrote an e-mail saying she told *Student* editor Jill Inkrott to: "1. Order a letter of apology from Aaron to Claire and to the French department. 2. Drop Aaron as a columnist. Really. This one, I think, requires a bigger response here."

The campus paper ran dueling letters. Strauss was given space for a reply to Sanders that got *tres* personal: "In fact, singling out sex from the vast array of materials that we do study reveals a fascination with it on the part of the column's author. Well, fine, to each his own."

Inkrott canned Sanders, and Heckler told him in an e-mail, "Your thoughtless determination to remain ignorant on getting the fuller picture ... has caused greater pain to a dedicated, careful, VALUABLE professor than you can possibly comprehend."

Sanders said he's a victim of ideological discrimination. Heckler and Inkrott said he was fired as an unpaid columnist not for his conservative opinions or any reporting errors, but for his "approach."

They said he did not see the movie before writing about it. But that's true for most reporting. Sanders didn't claim he saw it — he indirectly quoted students who did.

They said he should have warned Strauss that he was writing an opinion column before he quoted him. But Sanders said he asked Strauss to justify "excessive use of sexually explicit material."

"I thought it was apparent from the way I worded the questions that we were discussing opinions," Sanders said. "Either way, his answer to my question should not have changed depending on what type of piece I was writing. Right?"

Right.

Heckler and Inkrott said Sanders had a conflict of interest because he used his girlfriend as a source. But an *Enquirer* managing editor said if the story checks out, so what? Sanders said he used several sources.

Inkrott said Sanders did not act quickly to respond to complaints by Strauss. Sanders said Strauss refused to discuss it over the phone and was too busy to meet immediately.

Heckler said she has been unhappy with Sanders. "He has a stronger interest in being provocative and getting a response than thinking through an issue and making an intelligent argument."

But we're talking about a *student* newspaper — a place to learn. What lesson is Miami U. teaching? That only faculty members are valuable?

The plot is more tangled than a French movie with subtitles, but this much seems clear: Sanders' column angered Strauss. He raised hell, and Sanders was fired. Any more questions about faculty accountability?

Goldstein argued that *Ridicule* is a valuable part of the context of her course. "I do respect my students," she said. "I have made ample allowances for students who are uncomfortable with this."

She said she doesn't know why Sanders was fired. "He shouldn't be punished for his beliefs. He shouldn't be censored."

Critics say *Ridicule* is all about the power of words. And it looks like the faculty got the last word on Sanders: Off with his head.

Ridiculous.

No excuse for
Demagoguery 101

Professor Clinton Hewan is very outspoken. He once advocated stalking and killing a police officer. According to one of his students at Northern Kentucky University, he blames terrorist attacks on the United States on terrorism *by* the United States.

Although born in Jamaica, Dr. Hewan is a U.S. citizen, and that guarantees him the right to spout ridiculous nonsense.

But nothing gives him the right to inflict his far-left, anti-American political views on tuition-paying students, at taxpayer expense. Where do students go when they discover their course on International Politics is a misguided tour of the professor's fermented political whine cellar?

NKU sophomore Steve Fritsch has taken classes with Dr. Hewan in the NKU Political Science Department. "Dr. Hewan's statements in class are sometimes shocking," he wrote.

"He has a bias against 'white America' and says the problems of the African-American community are a result of racism. ... He often criticized Republicans and conservative thought and never missed a chance to call President Bush 'stupid' and a 'fool,' and even once called Vice President Cheney an 'evil man.' He has said in class that 'capitalism is evil,' and he routinely defends and promotes socialism. Also, he has said more than once that terrorism against the U.S. is a result of America's own form of terrorism against the poorer nations of the world."

That's high-octane gas, not political science. But Mr. Fritsch believes Dr. Hewan has every right to speak his mind. "However, Dr. Hewan's harsh anti-American rhetoric comes not without a price. The price is what students (and for many, their parents) are paying NKU in tuition."

He feels cheated and robbed.

"Dr. Hewan's class is not objective and not fair and balanced. During his classes, Dr. Hewan attempts to force his ideological beliefs on his students and tries to either suppress or ridicule any view contrary to his own."

I called Dr. Hewan. "I have no idea what you are talking about," he said before hanging up. "I don't speak to the press. Speak to the president if there is a complaint."

So I did. NKU President James Votruba said, "Academic freedom was created to let faculty members pursue the truth without worrying about their jobs. You will always have a few faculty members who take advantage of it. Abuse by a few is the price you have to pay to create an atmosphere where the many can push the frontiers of knowledge."

Good point. Better to suffer a few nutty professors than adopt chilling speech codes that are demanded by liberals on some campuses.

But the American Association of University Professors says freedom comes with responsibility. It says professors "should exercise restraint," "show respect for the opinions of others" and "be careful not to introduce into their teaching controversial matters which have no relation to their subject."

Such as "Dick Cheney is evil," perhaps.

Dr. Hewan was sanctioned by NKU's Faculty Senate two years ago for saying that the family of a man killed by a Cincinnati cop should "quietly stalk that S.O.B. and take him out." President Votruba said at the time, "The irresponsibility of these remarks is indefensible." Dr. Hewan apologized.

But he's still teaching four classes of International Politics and Political Science each semester, with 25 to 45 students in each class.

"There's no question he's a figure who draws stronger reactions on both sides of the spectrum," said NKU Provost Rogers Redding.

NKU officials have drawers of letters about Dr. Hewan. NKU collects student evaluations of professors as a management tool, but students never see the results.

The professors' grades should be made public so students can steer clear of the Frankenfaculty — or sign up, if that's their choice. Dr. Hewan does have admirers.

All universities should try harder to weed out incompetents and frauds who bully students with their personal political rants. President Votruba urged students to take complaints to the department chair. "Say, 'I don't like this,' and if others feel the same way, take them too," he said.

Dr. Redding said enough complaints can lead to discipline and removal, even for tenured professors like Dr. Hewan.

Steve Fritsch has voiced his complaint: "The amount of college tuition is already high enough without having to put up with these kinds of professors and the rhetoric they base their class on."

He's outspoken, too.

Bush won't flinch

In the early laps of his 2000 race for president, George W. Bush made a pit stop in Cincinnati. But I can't remember his speech.

On the way from his hotel to Memorial Hall, something happened that crowded out the rest of the evening like a fat man in the middle seat on a flight to L.A.

Sitting an arm's length away in a bouncing SUV, I asked him if his campaign promise of tax cuts was empty talk like his father's pledge of "no new taxes." I think I used the phrase, "read my lips," which is probably as popular around the Bush family as saying, "no controlling legal authority" at a Gore reunion.

He fixed me like a bug under glass with a stare that can only be described with an adjective from a Western novel: "steely."

I can't remember his answer that well, but I know it was simple, cold and straight as ice water. "Because I will do it." Period.

This year when I filed my IRS-1040, I found a nice bonus of tax cuts. He did it.

I saw the same steely resolution in his speech on Thursday night. But the president has changed a little. There was less bounce in his heels as he replied to the double-dare questions. He was respectful. Gracious. Composed. He refused to be baited or taunted. He was go-to-war serious.

He called the bluff of the ridiculous appeasers on the United Nations Security Council. He has played their game like a guy sitting in on dealer's choice poker. France and Germany keep changing the wild cards from deuces to one-eyed jacks.

But now Bush has the deal. Nothing's wild and he holds all the aces. Either Saddam has disarmed or he has not. Anyone who claims he has is immediately exposed as a liar and a cheat.

And Bush will keep his promise to disarm Saddam — because it's the right thing to protect our nation. He won't wait for a hall pass from the U.N.

Another thing Bush said that night in Cincinnati is a message for the anti-war protesters who can't see the plain truth: "I'm not about polls and focus groups." Protest all you want. We have a leader, not a weather vane. We have a president.

Besides, a lot of what I hear from the protesters sounds like bitter whine from fermented sour grapes.

Once upon a time we hated Nixon because we hated the war. Some of us who protested even thought we hated our country.

But now, I hear protesters who hate the war and their own country — because they hate the president.

Most of them said nothing about Kosovo. Europe couldn't shoot a rabid dog in its own backyard — and now we're supposed to wait for their permission to kill the snakes in our garden? I don't think so.

At least the people who hated Clinton were honest about their ample reasons.

Never mind, though, because Bush will do what has to be done, as sure as he cut taxes. The protesters are the mice that roar in the media, but the rest of the country knows what has to be done.

It goes back to a second-grade classroom in the Emma E. Booker Elementary school in Sarasota, Fla. Bush was listening to the children reading a lesson, when someone leaned over and whispered in his ear, "A second plane hit the second tower. America is under attack."

Some people just don't get it. But we are going to war because of what happened on that morning, Sept. 11, 2001 —— to make sure those kids in that classroom don't grow up in a world of terror.

Nobody wants war. But read my lips: President Bush will not back down. Thank God.

The anti-Clinton lie-brary

Ordinary taxpayers who tour the White House are herded behind ropes like cattle in a five-star stockyard. They're told, "Don't touch the historic lamps that Hillary threw at Bill."

OK, so they don't say it exactly that way, but you get the message: "Hands off." Only a small part of the White House is open for tours — like having an open house in your mudroom. It makes you wonder: What are they doing behind those locked doors?

A report last June by the GAO, thick as a Mason phone book, tells us. And it sounds like a Who concert at an *Animal House* toga party.

When the Bush team finally got the keys to the White House from the Clinton mob two years ago, they found: drawers glued shut, broken locks, wrecked furniture, chairs that had broken arms and legs, stains and cigar burns, large holes in walls, piles of pencil shavings, offices "extremely trashed," a dozen missing historic doorknobs, stolen presidential seals and TV remotes, 26 missing cell phones, more than 100 damaged phones, dozens of prank phone messages and obscene "greetings," computer and power cords ripped from walls and 62 keyboards with the "W" keys pried off.

The GAO interviewed hundreds of White House staffers and concluded that some of the vandalism was criminal. The Clinton gang said it was "normal wear and tear."

The report says the worst damage was in the offices for Vice President Al Gore and first lady Hillary Clinton.

Democrats adamantly denied it at the time. And President Bush was graceful enough to let them. But the GAO lays it out in sickening detail.

Why bring it up now? Because the Clintonistas desperately want us to forget it so they can rewrite history. The same liberals who hated Nixon for 20 years demand amnesty for their disgrace.

Not gonna happen.

While Mr. Clinton spends $200 million on his presidential library in Little Rock, another group is raising money for another Clinton monument almost next door.

"Our Counter Clinton Library will be a permanent thorn in the side of the Clintons as they try to hide and distort their anti-American, anti-family, anti-military legacy," says the Web site, www.counterclintonlibrary.com.

It will include the Hillary Hall of Shame, the Grifters Gallery, the National Insecurity Hall, Pardons for Dollars, Department of Domestic "Affairs" and the Exit Room, which will eventually show how the White House looked after the Clinton juveniles trashed it.

"The so-called mainstream media, which gave the Clintons a pass for all their misbehaviors while they were in office, are certain to let Bill and Hillary get away with lying about their misdeeds now, too," says the Web site, which says it is "Dedicated to presenting the TRUE Clinton legacy."

They have a point. Bill Clinton's Library will not be in the same time zone with the ugly truth.

The GAO reported a "terrible smell" in one White House office after the Clintons left. I think it was the Oval Office.

May 17, 2002

Jimmy Carter:
A world champion buttinsky

The blue book on Jimmy Carter says he was a lemon as a president, but has great resale value as one of the best used presidents.

That's not really fair. He has been lousy at both.

He gets more mileage out of a tool belt than Tim Allen. By showing up to hammer some two-by-fours together at Habitat for Humanity home-building sites, Mr. Carter has achieved sainthood among journalists, who are easily impressed by power tools, skilled trades and anyone who can do something besides talk about doing something.

I say, "Big deal."

Where was Jimmy Carter when *my* basement flooded?

I'll tell you where he was. He was meddling in some third-world sinkhole like the champion buttinsky he has always been.

Mr. Carter must be aware that he is no longer in charge of U.S. foreign policy and scheduling the White House tennis courts, but he seems to be doing his best to keep the rest of the world from finding out.

He has meddled everywhere from Baghdad to Toenail, Miss., wherever ignorant, backward people struggle to hold fair elections — such as Florida.

Now he's in Cuba, chumming with one of the last unembalmed Stalin groupies, Fidel Castro. Fidel has more political prisoners than Mr. Carter has teeth, and he shares biological weapons with terrorists who could use them to kill people whose only crime was voting for Jimmy Carter.

And when he's not on some grandiose mission to cozy up to our worst enemies, he's pontificating about the "mistakes" of the current president like some retired sidewalk superintendent who keeps wandering into the hard-hat area.

Mr. Carter has given heartburn to all of the presidents who had the misfortune to ignore his busybody advice. If you've ever wondered what ex-presidents talk about when they gather for funerals and awkward ceremonies, my guess is they ask each other, "How do you get rid of that pain in the neck Carter? — uh-oh, cheese it, here he comes now to tell us how to say 'nook-ya-ler.'"

That's why I think *USA Today* got it all wrong in a Page 1 Bush-whupping story on Monday,

"Former occupants haunt White House." Susan Page reported, "Presidents are members of one of the world's most exclusive fraternities, those who know firsthand the challenges of the Oval Office. You might think that an incumbent would see his predecessors as valuable resources, as repositories of knowledge and experience, as potential advisers and envoys."

No, I would not think that. I would think all presidents adopt the "Please, I would rather do it MYSELF!" policy, hoping that all ex-presidents have the class and good manners to shut up and go away.

President Reagan was no help to George Bush I. Obviously. And although Mr. Bush phones his son, he kept his lip zipped even when President Clinton was being impeached.

The glaring exceptions seem to be Mr. Clinton — who is an exceptionally needy special case with a raging addiction to himself — and Mr. Carter, who is — well, still a lemon.

Jan. 20, 2002

Weird play:
The war of the sexes

This is for men only. NO WOMEN ALLOWED.

Are they gone? OK, guys, close the door and shove a greasy engine block in front of it, because we are under attack.

Many of you are battle-scarred veterans of the war between the sexes. We have fought on the beaches, on the playgrounds, in cars, at parties, even on the way home from church. We've been through the trenches of hand-to-hand rhetorical combat with the unfairer sex. We know all too well the twilight struggle of the long cold war over forgotten anniversaries and accidental intrusions into her closet air space.

But now we face a new threat: A terrorist attack by radical fundamentalists who are determined to cripple our way of life with a kind of mental anthrax that spreads paralyzing fear and confusion among innocent men.

It may seem as harmless as a piece of cultural junk mail, but a play being shown in Cincinnati is releasing deadly spores that can turn men's brains to casserole.

Maybe some of you have seen the billboards as big as a beer truck. It may sound like a travelogue about Virginia, but it has no fishing, hunting, camping or places you'd like to take your family. Take my word for it.

Believe it or not, it's more than an hour of women sitting around talking about what they are sitting around on.

Sigmund Freud would be poleaxed. Not even he could have guessed that what women want is to go out on the town — and talk about their private parts.

Any man who tried this would be beaten with spiked heels, lynched with pantyhose, burned on a pyre of Redbooks and buried in an unmarked grave salted with potpourri.

A guy who even speaks the title of this play could wind up like Jerold Mackenzie, a manager at Miller Brewing(!) who was sued for sexual harassment in 1993 and lost his job for telling a joke from *Seinfeld,* about a word that rhymes with Regina. True.

ABC had to warn viewers about a show that included the same word.

But now it's OK to put it on billboards all over town to advertise a play that uses crude and vulgar synonyms to create "stark realism"?

If men did that, the stark realism is that they would be accused of coarsening our culture and encouraging perverts in raincoats.

Guys who watch the "Victoria's Secret Fashion Show" are branded "sickos" — by the same women who try to drag their husbands and boyfriends to a cozy theater where women talk like letters to "Hustler."

Go figure.

No, don't try, you will only get a brain seizure that will debilitate your reasoning so severely you might even think stuff like that is "art."

As Mark Twain said, "There is nothing more sophisticated than the pretentious swindles known as contemporary art." At least, he would have said that if he lived to be 167. But I digress.

Don't run off to join Johnnie Walker yet, men. There is good news.

Most women are not fundamentalist fanatics on a jihad against men. Many are peaceful.

And men are not as nuts as we thought we were when we tried to noodle out how women could defend a cheatin' heart in the White House that they would drive a stake through in their own house.

Consider this: Not even a mental contortionist can imagine any group of men sitting around discussing their privates. That's a good thing.

And most men would rather wear underwire intimate apparel to a poker game than go to the play that's showing at the Aronoff.

Finally, most men are not so paranoid they can't recognize the difference between scary censorship and harmless satirical criticism.

OK, men, now duck — and watch your backsides.

But only your own.

Reparations rally:
The check is in the U.S. mail

That national slavery reparations rally last Saturday fell as flat as gum on a shoe. They promised 1 million marchers — the mandatory media minimum for a protest in D.C. But they couldn't get half that many if they let Arthur Andersen count the crowd twice.

That's too bad. I was kind of hoping the whole reparations thing would sweep the nation like the West Nile virus. I figured it could turn out like one of those Oliver Stone movies: Pretty soon the conspiracy of oppression would get so vast it might even include me among the victims.

If the U.S. government caved in to the race hustlers and actually paid out a few billions to alleged distant descendants of slaves, the line outside the Capitol the next morning would stretch from "A" for aggrieved to "V" for victimized.

Pretty soon the U.S. government would have to declare bankruptcy and turn everything over to the courts, just like Enron. Highways, national parks, F-18s and nuclear submarines would be sold at auction to pay all the bankruptcy lawyers, and we'd all get class-action settlement checks for the many years we have been oppressed by the IRS — about $1.23 after the legal fees, I suppose.

Once the reparations slot machine started paying out jackpots, next in line would be the Indian tribes. If people who have never been closer to Africa than "The Lion King" can collect for something that happened 130 years ago, I'd say the Shawnees have a pretty good claim on repossessing Ohio and Kentucky, and maybe both Dakotas if we could get them to take them.

Then the South would rise again to claim reparations for the Civil War. The settlement could run into the billions just for punitive damages awarded to all those generations of boys named "Bobby Lee."

Cincinnati would get in line to claim reparations for all the damage done by the boycott, riots and the feral youths who gave the Black Family Reunion a big black eye.

A separate lawsuit by "Victims of the Cincinnati Bengals" could recover the enormous costs for all the pain and suffering of rooting for a losing team for an entire decade.

And that could lead to the biggest class-action lawsuit in history: Taxpayers vs. The Great Society.

Hard-working, middle-class taxpayers have been gouged for trillions to fund failed welfare and social programs perpetrated by liberal politicians.

Exhibit A is Richard King, the deadbeat dad sentenced to 27 months last week for having 10 kids with seven different mothers, and failing to pay more than $100,000 in child support.

How about some reparations for being forced to support slackers like that?

And what about reparations for all the other victims of society and circumstance: drug addicts, hookers, convicts, homeless guys and Al Gore?

Where do they get in line for a check?

I suppose it's insane to make people pay for something they had nothing to do with, such as slavery. But that's why we have courts to sort out the most lunatic ideas — and make them into laws.

Imagine This

Imagine no John Lennon. It's easy if you try. No more insipid platitudes. From that annoying guy. You may say I'm a dreamer. But I'm not the only one. I hope someday you'll join me. In a world that knows right from wrong.

Imagine this: Right after the Sept. 11 — the day the world shrank — Clear Channel sent out a list of insensitive songs that were banned from its 1,200 radio stations, including eight in Cincinnati.

No kidding.

These sensitivity police are the same people who hired "Bubba the Love Sponge" to dump toxic waste in Cincinnati. They are the corporate executives who promote shock jocks whose tongues should be scrubbed by a Haz-Mat team in orange plastic suits. They are the promoters who decorate billboards with stuff you can't explain to your kids without blushing like a stoplight.

Could it be that *these people* had a morality seizure?

It's like finding rules for towel-snapping etiquette posted in the junior high boys' locker room. Bad taste, perhaps, but if it wasn't for bad taste, they'd have no taste at all.

Clear Channel denied "banning" anything, and seemed offended to be accused of attempted decency.

There were mandatory protests about "censorship." The "ban" list included John Lennon's peace song "Imagine." Sacrilege! On stations that play oxymoronic "classic rock" it's almost a religious hymn.

I was blissfully ignoring it all. Just another woolly caterpillar in the Farmer's Almanac of signs that the coming winter is going to be unseasonably weird. Congress sharing bipartisan gas masks. Harvard bringing back the ROTC. And WEBN having "sensitivity" cramps.

But then those lyrics kept repeating in my head and I realized: They accidentally got it right.

I loved the Beatles so much I was the first kid in fifth grade to get a Beatle haircut. I listened to Sgt. Pepper until my brain rotated at 33 1/3 rpms. John Lennon was my hero.

But if any song is yanked after Sept. 11, I'd nominate "Imagine."

It's the antiquated anthem of moral relativity. The theme song for existential futility. Background Muzak for a generation that thinks nothing is evil except people who believe evil exists. A dirge of stumbling pacifist defeat.

Listen to it closely. It's not a song about peace. It's a song about emptiness. A world in which there is nothing worth fighting for. No heaven. No hell. No hope. No faith. No good. No bad. Nothing. Only empty sky.

And these days, that rock won't roll.

Right and wrong have never been more obvious. There are so many things to fight for, we don't know where to start the list. Is A for airlines or anthrax?

From where I stand, there's a new moral clarity as crisp and vivid as an October morning after a frost.

Like the day I met my friend Karl for lunch. He was leaving Monday to serve his country, called up from the Army Reserves for a year of active duty.

We talked about his plans to spend the afternoon with his son. We told him how much we admired him for driving into the storm clouds while the rest of us run for cover. We talked about how fast a year speeds by in our bland, ordinary lives.

But I could tell he was already missing his wife and kids. Each hour was suddenly measured in moments to be treasured later, miles away from home, dragged unexpectedly into the cyclone.

While we fret about what's on the radio, thousands of Karls among us have been plucked away, summoned on short notice to defend America and protect us all. They're riding to meet evil on the outskirts of civilization, with no guarantee that they will come home.

Imagine that.

Is that art or a joke?

My favorite Cincinnati joke is the one about two sheriff's deputies standing at the Mapplethorpe exhibit back in 1989 at the old Contemporary Arts Center. The first one asks, "So, whaddya think? Is that art?"

The second thinks awhile, then replies: "I dunno. I've never seen Art with his clothes off."

Now Cincinnati has a new $35 million arts center — the Lois & Richard Rosenthal Center for Contemporary Art — and the taxpayers who contributed $10 million to build it were thanked with another poke in the eye. On opening night, a Chinese performance artist in a police uniform, with a Doberman on a leash, walked on an American flag.

Was it art — or just a bad joke?

"Performance art can trigger a wide range of emotions," assistant curator Matthew Distel explained. "Some is deliberately provocative to stimulate conversation and thinking."

It stimulated me to think some nitwit deliberately insulted our nation and our city and the soldiers and cops who protect the rights of artists who perpetrate imbecilities in the name of free expression.

Distel said the "flag desecration issue" was discussed with artist Zhang Huan before Saturday's opening-night performance. But, "I don't think he would have understood that as a gesture of disrespect."

I guess that makes us even. Huan doesn't understand America, and most Americans don't understand contemporary art.

I admit I am clueless. But from what I gathered, it has a lot to do with pictures of naked people.

During my tour of the empty museum on Monday, I saw some pretty weird stuff that pretends to be "art". And it did make me think: Gee, if I hang a disco ball from the ceiling and call it art, will some "ahrts" patron with ocean-deep pockets and a wading-pool mind buy it?

What about that "artist" who creates "schizophrenic" pictures of someone cooking and eating human body parts? Shouldn't someone introduce him to the Chinese artist dressed in a "suit" of raw pot roasts? Wouldn't that be "performance art?"

How about those plywood tepees with portholes and artificial turf?

Is that art?

"That's the right question to ask," said deputy director Andree Bober. "We're here to provide a forum to ask, 'What is art?' We're not here to provide the answers."

And that made me think: That's a cool idea.

From one angle, the new arts center looks like a children's museum for demented adults only. From another, it looks like a hole in the fence where we can slip through occasionally to test the boundaries of our freedom of expression.

I'm in favor of that.

But gratuitously insulting the taxpayers who paid for it is still stupid.

So here's a new joke:

Two cops are standing at the Rosenthal center on opening night, watching a Chinese guy walking his dog on an American flag. The first one says, "Whaddya think. Is that art?"

The second one says, "No. It looks more like felony fraud by some bonehead impersonating an artist."

Back roads

A moving experience

When I arrived in Cincinnati nearly 10 years ago, with a full tank of attitude and a stick-figure picture of the city, a woman in the newsroom asked me what changes I would make in the *Enquirer* editorial pages.

"For starters," I said, "some of the syndicated columnists in our stable are ready for the glue factory, and then — "

"They won't let you do that," she said, shaking her head sadly, like a doctor delivering a tragic diagnosis.

I took it as a personal challenge. For nearly 10 years, I've tested the boundaries of the invisible fences in Cincinnati, with only occasional "mild corrections" that were no worse than holding onto live jumper cables hooked up to a moving cement truck.

It's been a heckuva ride.

I found out it's amazing what "they" will let you get away with in Cincinnati if you don't mind flying sparks and occasional shock treatments.

I have been blessed with a team of creative, talented professionals, an open-minded editor and a publisher who encouraged us to crank the voltage dial into the red zone.

Results were immediately apparent.

In my first week on the job, I was summoned to the *Enquirer's* Diversity Committee court to explain our felony opinions and misdemeanor political incorrectness.

Several civic-minded readers offered to take up a collection to put me on the next bus back to Arizona.

And that was *before* some Clintonistas decided I was like Ken Starr, but without all his charm.

I was testing the hypothesis that people do not stop reading editorial pages because they are too danged exciting. And the experiment worked. Mostly. I wrote some boneheaded opinions that should have been recalled like Firestone tires. But letters to the editor — the heartbeat of an opinion page — steadily increased from anemic dozens to healthy hundreds.

And we had fun.

I hope the opinion pages are spicier. I hope we encouraged positive changes in a city I love.

But I have to be honest: In the long, distinguished history of the *Cincinnati Enquirer,* I was only making footprints in the sand at low tide.

And after hundreds of endorsement interviews, thousands of editorials and what feels like eleventy billion brain-numbing meetings, I'm ready for a new beach.

Starting today, I am no longer associate editor of the opinion pages, the Sunday Forum, letters, cartoons, syndicated columns, editorials, crank calls, pickets and threats.

I am now a fool-time columnist. On Sundays, Wednesdays and Fridays, I will write personal columns in this space. It's my dream job — a chance to annoy people three times as often.

It's a chance to get off the bus that is loaded with the editorial board and all the luggage of *Enquirer* opinions, and climb on a Harley — more maneuverable, faster and more fun, but a bit more risky because there's nobody else to blame when I wipe out in a ditch. And I will.

It's a chance to let my curiosity off its leash and see what it digs up and brings back to the porch.

For the record: There is no sinister conspiracy to turn the news section to the right or yank the editorial wheel to the left. Anyone who has read my columns knows I am contrarian and conservative, but my opinions won't influence news coverage any more than a salmon swimming upstream influences a river.

If the idea of Peter Bronson three times a week gives you hives, I recommend aspirin and a dose of Maureen Dowditol. But if you like my Sunday Forum columns, I hope you will come along to the Metro section. It will be a heckuva ride.

I can't wait to find out what "they" won't let me do here.

The ghosts of Gettysburg

Gettysburg is not what it used to be. But then again, it is. It all depends on where you look.

On Veterans Day I was drafted to join a vanload of local Civil War buffs and cigar smokers for a poker and politics road trip eight hours and 130 years away.

Joining us there was syndicated columnist Walter Williams, who was good at all of the above.

As for me, I'm no historian, I choke on stogies and I never did see any one-eyed jacks or a lady with an ax. But I saw the Civil War in a whole new way. And I saw two different Gettysburgs.

On the drive-through blur, it's a shrine to tourism. Robert E. Lee's Southern Fried Chicken serves hush puppies and artificially flavored history across the street from lichen-dusted, stone-eyed statues of long-dead Civil War heroes.

You can buy real Civil War bullets that might have missed someone famous. Abe Lincoln shakes hands with an awkward tourist like some smarmy politician running for President of Bronze Statues.

Marching columns of shops sell little plastic bags of uniform buttons, shards of broken weapons and other grave-robber relics that still scatter the ground where 51,000 Americans were killed, wounded or missing.

That's something it's easy to forget — both sides were Americans who fought and died far from home. On American soil. For American ideals.

Thousands who died in the orchards and pastures and wheat fields around Gettysburg were dumped into open trenches after bloating in the July sun during the three-day battle. Later, they were dug up and buried again in a cemetery, as workers rifled their pockets in a grisly inventory of watches, love letters and other future souvenirs.

That's Gettysburg, 1994.

But get out and walk on the battlefield under a moonless sky at midnight, and it's once again a quiet little farm town that was caught in the crossfire of history on July 1, 1863, just long enough to decide the fate of our nation.

They say the winners of wars get to write the history, and that's what we were taught when I was growing up, the victors' version: The Civil War was fought over slavery. The North was right, the South was wrong. A house divided against itself cannot stand, blah, blah, end of story, test on Friday. Next subject.

But that's not what I heard from the ghosts on the battlefield.

Out there in the silent darkness, flat rocks make natural tombstones at the "Highwater Mark" of the South, where Pickett's charge surged like a crashing wave and receded, dragging the Confederacy back down in an undertow of sorrow, blood and defeat.

Out there, if you are still and quiet long enough, things move on the fringe of your vision. A collective sigh of sadness, fear and pain from thousands of lost spirits is close enough to touch, as real around the edges as the black hole in a brick barn where a cannon ball crashed through more than a century ago.

If you listen, the ghosts say God was on both sides, and the war isn't over.

They say Mississippi farm boys barely old enough to shave didn't march their shoes into dust all the way to the strange, rolling hills of Pennsylvania to protect some plantation owner's slave property.

They say Texans and Virginians didn't march straight ahead into the thunder and lightning of Union cannons because they were fighting to keep other men in chains.

I suppose that when the shooting starts, each side looks for a moral cause to cling to. Abolishing slavery was better for the North than preserving some vague federal Union that dissolved into empty maps of the Western prairies.

But on the other side, the threat of losing liberty to that Union was cause enough. The South fought to preserve a nation founded on individual freedom spelled out in the Tenth Amendment: "The powers not delegated to the United States by the Constitution, nor prohibited by it to the States, are reserved to the States respectively, or to the people."

Today, the Tenth Amendment might as well be buried under a marble monument. The Union is a government of, by and for group needs and central control.

If abolishing slavery was the best thing that came from the Civil War, the tyranny of federal government that threatens to make slaves of us all was the worst.

I don't think government-dependent Americans today are even the same species of self-reliant humans who settled the country and fought the Civil War. But we are still fighting the same battles for freedom.

Now and then, as on Nov. 8, Americans fire on government's Fort Sumter with ballots, not bullets.

The ghosts of Gettysburg say there's still some rebel in all of us.

Poets of the pickup nation

Back in the day when I was a Hippie who looked like the Zig-Zag Man in a Hawaiian shirt and torn Levis, I thought I could find the secret Meaning of Life on the back of a Moody Blues album.

The thrashing guitars, swooping bass lines and drums that thud like waves pounding the edge of the world still sound good. But the plaintive vocals have lost their exotic mystery. All that weepy wailing about the end of the world sounds as dated as "bummer" and "faaaar out, maaaan."

The Moody Blues had a gift for insinuating deep meanings they couldn't deliver. It got so bad they turned on their overwrought fans with a song that said, "I'm just a singer in a rock'n'roll band." It was like having the Pope tell thousands on Vatican Square, "Hey, don't ask me, I just work here."

I should have known you can't find the meaning of life in rock 'n' roll. For that, you need country. It's America's music.

The British ripped off the blues. Even the French can do jazz. But nobody does country like our country.

The picnic of fiddles and mandolins, banjos and guitars sounds like our American family at a reunion under a shade tree in July. The roots spread out from the Appalachians to the Rockies, from Texas to Tennessee.

But they curl and die as they get near the elitist coasts.

That's because country clings to the simple honesty of the heartland the way crops cling to soil.

I fell in love with country while I was painting my house and heard George Strait singing about "The Chill of an Early Fall" on the radio. There's something about working outdoors that fits country music the way pointy-toe boots fit a rodeo cowboy.

Country is the poetry of ordinary people. The songs and deep universal truths are spun out of the plain cotton of casual remarks you'd hear over a Bud after framing a house.

And nearly all of it has a moral rhythm that's as "country" as steel guitars. There's cheatin' and lyin' and drinkin' to drown the hurtin'. But there's always a price to pay for "doin' her wrong." The rules are as straight as fresh-plowed furrows.

That's why the Dixie Chicks are as popular as a flat tire on a Friday night.

The lazy rocking-chair drawl of Randy Travis sounds like screen doors and crickets on a porch at sundown. He sings about the sad "reasons I cheat," but he also sings about fidelity: "On the other hand there's a golden band, that reminds me of someone who wouldn't understand."

Some of his stuff is "as honest as a robin on a springtime windowsill."

"I keep waiting for you to forgive me. You keep saying you can't even start. And I feel like a stone you have picked up and thrown, to the hard rock bottom of your heart."

When Travis and Strait sing about the Lord, it's not Styrofoam-peanut filler. It's full of meaning I never found in the Moody Blues.

America's music is the simple cowboy code: Faith. Family. And love of country.

The symphony of springtime

A robin blows his urgent whistle like a Cracker Jack toy, "Wake up, Wake up, the light has returned," and so it begins: God's greatest masterpiece, a spring morning.

It can dawn in mist, shrouded behind a veil like the face of a bride, or crackle with sunshine that sparkles like the eyes of a happy child. Sometimes it tiptoes into the bedroom and tugs our sleeve. Other days it crashes into the room in a splash of bright yellow cymbals.

No painting in any museum can match it. No sculpture compares. No symphony can thrill us like the overture of springtime.

In the opening notes, the grass sheds its gray and brown winter jacket and emerges in a deep jade green so rich you can almost hear it grow like the sound of a bass fiddle played with a bow.

The daffodils rise to their feet in crowded clusters and blow their little cornets while the birds play soft flutes and woodwinds in the trees.

On a morning like this, the smell of fresh-cut grass and flowering trees on the breeze is like catnip that makes us want to run and leap and curl our stretched toes deep in the lawn. We want to lie in the grass and drink up the soft sun that rubs a loving hand through our hair. We want to lie back and close our eyes and just listen to the symphony of God's music that surrounds us. Each day is a separate masterpiece, completely different, never to be duplicated or repeated.

Springtime in the Arizona desert is stealthy and subtle like a flirting smile. The palo verde trees that have no leaves turn yellow in their best imitation of a forsythia. Sage and cactus on the desert floor turn a bewitching color of dusty grayish green, and laurel fills the air with the clean, fresh incense of heaven itself.

But spring is fleeting and muted in the desert. Here in Ohio, it's a full-season concert, played fortissimo.

In the dark scribble of mist-shrouded black tree trunks and limbs, the gangly redbud in lavender tights does its ballet in the forest.

Old lady magnolias in their pink and white splashy housedresses fill the air with a flowery sweet cologne like a grandmother's hug.

Flowering crab trees get as fat and fluffy as long-haired cats.

Tulips spring up with reds and yellows so true they would embarrass the oils on Van Gogh's palette.

And the soft chalky pastels of Easter eggs hide in the grass like secret messages to remind us what

128

it's all about. Rebirth. Renewal.

Resurrection.

It is entirely possible to enjoy spring and never pause to consider how God's music tells us a story about his Son.

We can look at the tulips, and never see the blood-red cup that was passed from lip to lip on Passover.

We can smile at the playful daffodils and never see the gold trumpets that announced, "He is Risen!"

We can see the beauty all around us, and never imagine the Creator who made it all and loves us enough to bring us the miracle of new life after a cold, sterile, colorless coma of winter.

We can see a trilling stream and feel the gentle caress of spring rain and never stop to think about the living water that God wants us to drink for refreshment and joy.

But it's like looking at a great painting and seeing only dots and dabs of dried paint.

It's the difference between a rhyme and great poetry.

It's the difference between a headline and the story God tells in the beauty all around us.

Each spring morning is a renewal of His love that lights the world.

The road not taken

It was paved in old blacktop like any ordinary country road, framed with arching, lush July trees that leaned their heads together to whisper in a conspiracy with the breeze. The white lines down the middle rose gently to a soft horizon that emptied into a deep blue sky.

For some reason, it beckoned.

Unlike hundreds of nameless roads that pass like the repeating background scenery in a cartoon chase, this one promised to wind through places of mystery and discovery, just over that seductive, curved hill.

I passed it twice and never made the easy turn to find out what was on the other side of that hill. Even on vacation, I was in a hurry. "I'll come back when I have more time," I lied to myself.

But sometimes, when I think of that vacation, I think of the place I didn't go. Down that road.

For all of us who are locked on the white lines ahead of us, too busy getting from Point A to Point B in a ruler-straight line to go down that beckoning country road, there is someone who does — and lucky for us, he takes us along by writing about his discoveries with Rand McNally's attention to detail and Huck Finn's innocent wonder.

William Least Heat-Moon takes the road less traveled. While the rest of us won't stop without a farmhouse near, he explores blank spots on the map.

"At home I have an old highway atlas, worn and rebound, the pages so soft from a thousand thumbings they whisper as I turn them," he writes at the beginning of his new book, "River Horse." "Every road I've ever driven I've marked in yellow, the pages densely highlighted, and I can now say I've visited every county in the contiguous states except for a handful in the Deep South, and those I'll get to soon."

That's 3,200 counties: 2,900 highlighted, about 300 to go.

"I've been interested since I was about 10 years old to find another way to see America," Mr. Heat-Moon said on Monday at the Mercantile Library, during a visit to Cincinnati.

In his first book, "Blue Highways," he explored America from the back roads — the little blue lines on the map that the rest of us do our best to avoid.

This time, he crossed the country by water: 5,000 miles and 506 pages of rivers from the Atlantic to the Pacific, in a boat "the size of a 1957 Cadillac."

Big car. Small boat. Lake Erie was "six hours of unrelieved terror," he said.

He stood under the tall windows and high ceilings of the historic Mercantile, surrounded by old books on China and Peru and the North Pole like so many ancient cave paintings by long-dead explorers, and told us there is still an unexplored America.

All the yellow plastic franchise playpens on all the interstates haven't killed it yet. There are rivers and streams and mountains that still remember Lewis and Clark.

Boxed and packaged in a 19-inch picture tube, America looks homogenized, a Dockers nation that talks like an anchorman, with no detectable accent. We think alike, look alike and act alike, hurtling down the highways in colored jelly beans from the same bowl, stopping to refuel at brightly lit anthills of plastic, glass and steel, as seen on TV, each exactly like the others at every convenient exit.

Mr. Heat-Moon, whose name comes from his Osage Indian grandfather, was here to tell us that is the mythical America. The Huck Finn nation lives, just over a hill. The sanitized, two-dimensional life on the ruler's edge is a dream that is dreaming us.

Someone asked him how America looks from its rivers, compared to the view from meandering blue highways. "The answer is the book itself," he replied.

I can't wait to read it, but that's not why I was there.

When my father died, he left me two antique, cane-bottomed kitchen chairs and his beloved copy of "Blue Highways." I never knew if it was by design or default. It doesn't matter.

They make perfect bookends.

At one end of our quest is where we live, gathered with our loved ones around the hearth of our kitchen. We have "living rooms" and "family rooms," but real families do their living in their kitchens — sharing meals, setbacks and victories, welcoming friends, planning the future, working out problems.

At the other end are all the blue highways, the roads that take us off the beaten path to our dreams and discoveries — just over that hill.

The night we saw an angel

...and other Christmas stories

The less you get, the more you have

Even after 40 years of eggnog, carols and the dreamy scent of evergreens indoors, a few Christmases still glow like little brass angels dancing over candles, as fresh as cookies left out for Santa.

The best ones confirm my unscientific theory that Christmas is subject to the law of all timeless designs: Less is more.

When I was 7, we had to move into town and leave our friends in the outskirts of a small city in Michigan. The house we moved into was tall and faded white like a stale wedding cake, older than the "McKINLEY SHOT" headline I found on a yellowed newspaper in a musty closet.

It was so cold that year, even in the time it took us to collect the milk from the box on the back porch, where the milkman left it before dawn, frozen crystals of white ice would push the little round cardboard caps right off.

Each day on our six-block walk to school, my two older sisters seethed with resentment at my undeserved good fortune to be born a boy. They envied my thick corduroys and described in chilling detail the needles of ice that tortured their bare legs. Girls wore dresses. No exceptions. Little brothers were an insufferable burden. No exceptions.

We had our own skating rink that year on the side of the house, right under a bay window where our Christmas tree was lit. I'm sure our new neighbors watched the project from behind their curtains, sniggering at our foolishness. But the joke was on them. It worked. We had the only family ice arena I ever heard of — proof of what a single mom can accomplish without a knowitall dad around to tell her why it won't work.

Years later, I learned we were raggedy poor that year. But at the time, I was 7, faithful to Santa, and blissfully ignorant of the starring role money plays in the Christmas pageant.

Another thing I discovered later: Although we didn't talk about it then, we all knew that house was haunted.

We moved in "as is," the furniture still warm from the dearly departed elderly owners. In the back of the pantry, we found a cookbook with recipes for strange poultices and mustard plasters. In the attic, we found a treasure in a leather and wooden box with gold lettering: "Magic Lantern." It

133

was a candle-powered, Model-T-era slide projector, complete with a little chimney. The white linen "screen" and hand-painted glass slides conjured scenes of kids in knickers flying red kites in a watercolor blue sky.

In the basement, in a dank room lit by clear light bulbs that could have been signed "Tom Edison," we found a cupboard full of Zud Soap. The stuff had lye in it, and cinder-like grit that made it feel like skin-burning sudsy sandpaper. It could scrub whitewalls right off the tires of our '58 Chevy.

And in nearly every room, we found the uneasy feeling of someone there when we thought we were alone.

One morning we came down and discovered all the tall candles in the house curled over like question marks. We blamed it on the Coal Furnace Monster in the basement, a fire-breathing, soot-belching beast that we never got the hang of feeding. Give it too little to eat and it would go out like a snuffed cigarette, demanding kindling to work again. Give it too much, and we had to open all the doors and windows when it was 10-below and still couldn't eat our ice cream before it melted.

But the Furnace Monster had to be stoked every night, which meant going down in that cold, creepy basement, darker than a coal miner's lung, where the ghosts patiently waited. Most of the time, my nearest sister treated me the way the warden treated prisoners in Cool Hand Luke: "What we got heah is a failyuh ta comYUNicate, boy — dry them there dishes again." My older sister was more aloof. Like Lex Luther, she let her henchsister handle the pest.

But they were kind to me when they needed help to feed the furnace monster. And they were more kind than I knew that Christmas, babysitting every chance they got to raise enough so the avalanche of bright presents would brush the bottom branches of our tree.

Santa came through with an erector set and a space station. But the Big Gift that stopped me in my tracks was a chair. Yes, Santa brought me grownup-size chair. The responsibility and pride of owning your own furniture at age 7 was so awesome, I didn't even stop to puzzle over the picture of chair legs sticking out of Santa's bag.

Besides, Santa knows all and he knew we needed a chair of our own that didn't seem sat-in by the previous owners. It became my reserved seat to watch the Three Stooges. My friends were very impressed. Anybody could have an erector set. I was the only kid in second grade who had his own chair delivered by Santa.

I even let my mean sisters use it. They asked politely, but smiled knowingly as if they were in on something.

But no ghosts were allowed.

I realize now that we didn't have much that year. But we had each other, and that's more than enough for the best Christmases.

Confessions of a shopaphobe

Don'tcha just love this time of year between the Thanksgiving and Christmas turkeys, when even the beer commercials look like Norman Rockwell illustrations and people walk around with silly grins and sparkling eyes, as if sniffing pine needles and staring at colored lights has a psychedelic effect.

The minimum adult requirement for roast turkey in America is two, but as nice as people act between dosages you'd think we'd eat it more often.

In grade schools, this is paste season. I can almost smell it. They start you on turkey tail-feather centerpieces and pilgrim hats and keep you pasting everything that can't paste you back, right on through the red-and-green paper chains for the Christmas tree.

I don't know what the cumulative effect of all that paste-handling is on American students. (Do test scores dip during paste projects?)

The way people feel this time of year, all swelled with goodwill and tipsy on holiday spirit, I was even ready to write a column without being negative. But then I checked the fine print in my Editorial Writer's Code and discovered that no holiday comment is allowed without adding something to make people feel guilty for being so happy (TV news has the same rule). So here it is:

There is a darker side to the holidays.

I'm not talking about the alcoholics, homeless people and wife beaters that liberals rediscover each Christmas and use like an antidote to good cheer.

I'm talking about a group that is completely ignored by society — outcasts whose tragic disability is painfully aggravated by every Christmas carol and scrap of tinsel: The shopping impaired.

Psychiatrists say the first step to overcoming a problem is admitting you have one, so let me confess mine. I have shopaphobia, a syndrome characterized by insecurity, fear of crowds, aversion to long lines and general depression following bouts of binge shopping.

My problem was less noticeable as a child, when I could go out at the last minute and buy Mom a half-gallon of Eau de Woolworth's that smelled like the flea-dip tub at a dog kennel.

We had an understanding: She wouldn't wear it and I wouldn't ask.

I even managed to limp through Christmases buying incredibly lame, last-minute gifts for my sisters. But by the time I was 17, gifts such as 101 Army Men, Spiderman comics and model cars ("We can build it together!") had worn thin and they were on to me. The payback came when they gave me 10 pounds of "Reduced" black bananas for my birthday. The house smelled like a monkey cage for a month. Even the whiff of a ripe banana still makes my skin crawl.

But it didn't stop me. I resorted to another shopaphobics ploy: "Going in." As in: "So what are you getting for Mom for Christmas? A new purse? Cool. Hey, howbout I go in with you? I have $1.57 if you don't mind change . . . "

If you've had a shopaphobic in your family, you may have been an enabler for "Going in." You may vividly recall how used you felt hearing about the gift "we" picked out.

But shopaphobics know no shame.

We will do anything to avoid actually going to a store and picking out a thoughtful gift.

We love those tacky cards that say, "I didn't have time to shop so here's a check that should help you buy your own." Then inside is some wiseacre line like, "Be sure to CHECK your wallet before going shopping." Hardy-har.

Our motto is, "It's the thought that counts," and we say it without thinking.

We're the ones who put the $1.89 shoe horn, complete with price tag, in the $5-limit "secret Santa" office exchange.

When someone opens our gift of nail clippers or a candle shaped like Snoopy, and gets that crestfallen, angry look of disbelief, we blurt out, "I can take it back" — and of course they always feel guilty and lie, "Noooo, it's just what I always wanted."

I've hit rock bottom. I gave my grandfather a carton of Winstons the year he got emphysema. I once considered slipping $10 bills in my kids' Christmas stockings ("Look — Santa left a tip for the milk and cookies!").

And I have committed the ultimate shopaphobe's sin: I once gave my wife a Dustbuster. Now I'm scared to spill anything. Every time someone turns it on the motor yells at me, "How could you!?"

So try to be kind to shopaphobics this year — make a list, in BIG block letters, and check it twice. Don't cut us any slack or you'll wind up with key chains that say "John Deere Tractors" and hygiene products under the tree.

As for me, I'm not waiting until the last minute this year. First thing tomorrow I'm going to ask my 4-year-old son if he will let me "go in" on that paper chain he's pasting together for his mother.

A few good Christmas traditions

Somewhere there is a place where fat, feathery snowflakes tumble gently from the sky in slow motion, where tangerines grow on fir trees and the air is rich with the perfume of pine needles and roasting turkey, where silence is broken by the tinkling chimes of little brass angels swirling graceful loops around a flickering candle.

I think it's the place where they bottle the sights, sounds and smells of 100-proof Christmas spirit, so we can pass it around once a year. Just a sip makes children swoon with delight at the sight of an unopened present, then stay up late into the night listening intently for the soft tap of reindeer hooves on roof shingles. A taste makes women tipsy with tearful joy at the everyday sight of their family gathered together, hands held in prayer before dinner. A few gulps can make grown men so giddy with goodwill they put on loud Santa Claus neckties and plunge into the mall crowds to go shopping for whole minutes at a time, bringing home gifts with "some assembly required" long into the Christmas dawn.

Christmas spirit goes with eggnog, sleigh-shaped cookies, logs in the fireplace, strings of red, green and blue lights, choir music and a splash of bubbly excitement. It causes euphoria, relaxation and — sooner or later — the uncorking of well-aged traditions.

For newlyweds, the first Christmas is like two speeding locomotives colliding in a train-wreck of rituals. He likes blinking lights. She prefers the "peaceful" lights that sit still. He likes his Country Christmas with Brenda Lee "Rockin' Around the Christmas Tree." She prefers Handel's Messiah, and wants to dash his Elvis tape in pieces like a potter's vessel.

He grew up with garish chrome shreds of plastic called "icicles" hanging from the family tree like Spanish moss. She winces and accidently vacuums them off the carpet where they have accidentally fallen when she accidentally shook the tree while he was carrying in another log.

And finally, when they get the Christmas train back on track, they adopt a permanent set of traditions. Hers.

Later on, the kids come along and choose their own careful rituals to throw on the Christmas fire like kindling — an ornament that must be hung just so, a bedtime story they have to hear, about some Christmas long past, before they were even candy canes on Santa's list.

And sometimes, chance rings the doorbell with traditions wrapped in red foil.

Ours includes The Falling Tree. It began on my side of the family — one of the few survivors of the marriage train-wreck. One Christmas morning, my sister's cat was somehow startled by the kind

137

of loud noise a new cap gun might make going off next to a cat's tail. He did what cats naturally do when crazed with terror: He climbed the nearest tree and, reaching the thinning top, made a mournful sound like a distant police siren that rose an octave as our Christmas tree slowly leaned drunkenly and crashed to the carpet like. . . a falling tree.

Over the years, the tradition has been revived with a twist: It always happens as we gather to admire our decorations, usually while guests are in the room.

Last year, after our traditional debate over the proper size of a tree, we selected one that was larger than usual. Sequoia-Size, with a waist like a Sumo wrestler.

And when we put it in our traditional too-small tree stand, I made the traditional mistake of saying, "Don't worry, it's steady."

It never wobbled or swayed. It stood patient, as solid as a tree statue, waiting for the precise moment of sneak attack. Then when a large crowd gathered to admire it, it slowly toppled to the carpet in a crash of ornaments and lights, like a skyscraper in an earthquake movie.

This year I argued again for a tree that could fall without setting off seismic shock waves that look like underground nuclear tests in China. But the wife wanted one even bigger than last year's, so we compromised — and did it her way.

Trees come and go, they fall like Christmases, with a clatter and crash of lights and presents, over too fast to change anything. So I try to enjoy it while it stands there: a thing of beauty, decorated with love, an evergreen spirit of joy that began when one little baby was born thousands of years ago, bringing hope to mankind that still swells in our hearts today.

Merry Christmas.

138

Christmas in a bottle

FROM: Benson Burner, vice president for research and development, Double-Secret Experimental Station, Proctoid & Grumble.

TO: Rich Suits, president of New and Improved! Products Division.

RE: Christmas Project.

FOR YOUR EYES ONLY — CLASSIFIED — TOP SECRET! Dear Mr. Suits:

It has been a good year. New and Improved! Clam Chowder Pringles did not meet expectations in the Cincinnati test market, but losses were offset by surprisingly strong sales in our California Division, where they were marketed as Fat-Free Sushi Rice Cakes.

I am sorry to report, however, that our efforts to reproduce a synthetic Christmas Spirit have been disappointing.

Our experiment with powdered mistletoe, red tights, artificial snow and genetically improved pine sap did produce a remarkably lifelike department-store Santa, but she scared the children. Our marketing team believes it may be decades before children and shoppers are ready for a lingerie model in a white beard who shakes like a bowl full of jelly.

Our experiment with flying reindeer has been indefinitely postponed to sort out the litigation and liability issues from that unfortunate incident near the airport.

It may be small consolation, but our analysis of our competitors indicates that our research, flawed as it is, remains at the frontier of efforts to find a substance that accelerates buying behavior and duplicates December sales levels over a 12-month period (code named "Christmas in a Can").

Hollywood had success with *It's a Wonderful Life* in 1946, but the best and brightest producers, actors and writers have not been able to duplicate it since then. Not even Bruce Willis.

Book publishers have had even less success. They have not produced a credible source of genuine Christmas Spirit since 1843, when Charles Dickens published *A Christmas Carol.*

The newspaper industry gave up years ago when it discovered that the fragile essence of Christmas cannot coexist in an atmosphere of concentrated cynicism.

Much to their dismay, advertisers have invested billions only to find that their best efforts often extinguish naturally occuring seasonal cheer and leave a bitter aftertaste of avarice. This tends to support our own hypothesis that undiluted commercialization may be incompatible with the warm feelings of generosity and kindness that generally accompany spontaneous Christmas joy.

And compared to our results, the broadcasting industry has suffered devastating setbacks in its attempts to fabricate surrogate family Christmas gatherings on sitcoms and other programming (see videotapes of *North Pole Survivor, King of Queens in Bethlehem, Buffy The Snowman Slayer* and *Jerry Springer: Too Hot for the Holidays*).

On a positive note, our field research involving scientifically controlled observations of behavior in our targeted demographics indicates measureable increases in Christmas spirit near Salvation Army kettles and in proximity to any child who believes in Santa Claus. We recorded high levels near some churches year round, and we're investigating claims that the source of pure Christmas Spirit may be linked to the birth of Christ in a manger 2,000 years ago.

Unfortunately, there is no consensus on the ingredients of Christmas spirit even within families, much less for a national market (see attachment "Focus Group Violently Disagrees on Colored Lights vs. White, Blinking vs. Non-blinking, Elvis vs. Handel, Artificial Trees, etc.").

Our conclusion: A synthetic version of Christmas Spirit will never substitute for traditional family recipes.

The night we saw an angel

The angels who scared the fleece out of those poor shepherds on the first Christmas Eve must have been pretty awesome. Bigger than the Goodyear blimp. Blinding white. Blowing trumpets that sounded like a marching band in a tornado.

"An angel of the Lord appeared to them, and the glory of the Lord shone around them, and they were terrified," the Bible says (Luke 2:9).

I believe it. I saw an angel once. She was pretty scary, too.

She looked exactly like my Aunt Merece, who had a tongue so rough it could strip the rust off a junkyard hubcap. When she got going, she could melt a snowman two blocks away and scold the hair off a dog. It was enough to put a blush on the face of a clock.

She wore those cat-woman glasses with rhinestones in the pointy corners. And she had on tall galoshes. Not boots. Galoshes with big metal latches. Her flowing robes were a scarf and a tweed overcoat. Her "trumpet" was a Winston.

"But the angel said to them, 'Do not be afraid. I bring you good news of great joy that will be for all the people.'" (Luke 2:10)

My angel said, "Get off your fat duff and go help your sisters." I was only in third grade, but I could tell she meant business.

The poor shepherds found "a baby wrapped in cloths and lying in a manger." I found a Pontiac in the driveway, packed with grocery sacks. There was a lot of stuff. Cake mixes, eggs, steaks, bread, hamburger, canned soups, ice cream and even candy. But we had plenty of room to put it away because our refrigerator was as cold and empty as King Herod's heart.

We had been living on a diet of mostly navy beans from a 50-pound burlap bag. Beans on bread. Bean soup. Baked beans. While other kids were all snug in their beds with visions of sugarplums dancing in their heads, we had beans in our dreams.

We opened the candy first, and our angel was OK with that. And then she took us sledding.

When we got to the park, we went down the hill a few times and she finally flicked away her cigarette and said, "What's the matter with you kids? Don't you know how to ride a sled?"

She grabbed a sled like a surfer running into the ocean, and dove off the hill head-first. We could not have been more amazed if she sprouted white feathered wings and rose up to greet a heavenly host singing "Jingle Bell Rock" with Vic Damone.

Then we picked up our jaws, grabbed our sleds and went head-first after her, flying downhill in a cloud of spraying snow. That night went down in family history as The Time Aunt Merece Taught us to Bellyflop.

I suppose Aunt Merece was just helping out her little sister who was struggling to raise three kids alone. Uncle Harve owned an IGA store, so maybe it was no big deal to her.

To us, it was a visit from an angel.

"Glory to God in the highest, and on earth peace to men on whom his favor rests," the angels told the shepherds.

I think it means each of us can be an angel to someone.

To order more copies of

Cincinnati...
For Pete's Sake

please go to
www.peterbronson.com

144